LITTLE BOOK OF
LAND ROVER

Foreword by Stephen Vokins

HISTORY OF
LAND ROVER

First published in the UK in 2007

© G2 Entertainment Limited 2015

www.G2ent.co.uk

Printed and bound in India by Imprint Press

ISBN 978-1-78281-292-0

Contents

Foreword

TAKE A WALK AMONG THE AMASSED vehicles on display at The National Motor Museum at Beaulieu and you'll see every kind of machine, from steam cars, to land speed record breakers, family cars to luxury cars and even famous cars. Some cars automatically catch your attention, but there is one very humble machine that most people walk by without so much as a glance. And that's a shame, because this little gem has every right to be celebrated as a monumental moment in the history of the motor-car. Made in 1947, it is a Land Rover. It's not just any Land Rover, however. A discreet number 4 on the front chassis cross-member gives a clue to its significance. This is Land Rover number 4: a pre-production prototype of the car that was destined, quite literally, to conquer the world.

Greatness wasn't planned into this car. In fact, it was only supposed to be a stop-gap car, designed to get the Rover Car Company back into production as soon as possible after the end of the war, at a time when the normal materials required for car manufacture, and in particular, steel, were still rationed and difficult to obtain. The Rover management, seeing the versatility offered by the Jeep, of which many, having been left behind at the end of the war, were now available to the private owner, decided to have a go at making their own 4-wheel drive car with its own go-anywhere ability, using aluminium for its body panels. The Land Rover, as it came to be known, was pitched at hill farmers, and aiming to match or improve on the Jeep's rugged qualities, had to be able to transport sheep, carry straw bales, pull carts and tow equipment. It also had to have power take-offs, and accommodate a plethora of bolt-on accessories. In other words, this little wonder had to be capable of any task its owner might set it. When launched, it was an immediate success, although the original intended customer base soon found they were competing with some unexpected purchasers: King George VI had one, as did Winston Churchill, and the Police and the Military were quick to realize the potential this remarkable vehicle possessed.

The Land Rover had arrived. That today's Defenders are still visually similar to this original says much about how right that 1947 car was. The Range Rover, Discovery and Freelander mod- els subsequently developed are all obvious descendants from this proud heritage and share much of the unique qualities of a Land Rover. This book maps the story of not just the cars, but also the company, through its highs and lows, and illustrates how, for many journeys, there is still only one machine of choice: the Land Rover.

BELOW Motoring historian Stephen Vokins with the National Motor Museum's Land Rover 4

Chapter 1

Introduction

RIGHT Freelander and Discovery on display

THIS IS THE STORY OF THE LAND Rover, a British institution, one that in its predominantly dark green livery is nearly as recognisable as the scarlet post boxes or London buses, or the old dark blue policeman's helmet. It was a victory of content over style, a triumph of functionality that over the years was paradoxically to become an icon of style. Setting the evolution of the Land Rover in context, a short history of the Rover car company is followed by an examination of the upsurge in its fortunes brought about by two brothers, Spencer and Maurice Wilks, who were also to be pivotal in the development of this vehicle. There are concise examinations of all the major Land Rover models as they have been created although there isn't enough space in this book to encompass every variant.

The story begins in the austere days

after the Second World War with the invention of the prototype Land Rover (which later came to be known as Series I) and its launch in 1948, followed by the Series II models from 1958 onwards and the Series III from 1971 to 1985.

Not content with having created the commercial off-road vehicle market out of nothing, the company repeated the

trick. From 1970, the company developed the luxury off-road market with its Range Rover, and proved that it could innovate as successfully at the top of the market as in the utilitarian field.

Later the original Land Rovers were replaced with the Ninety and One Ten models, which from 1990 were rebranded as the Defender. This name was allegedly dreamed up in a Boston bar although, given the company's military connotations, it sounds a logical choice.

A year earlier, the company had launched the Discovery as its riposte to the Japanese invasion of the newly emergent lifestyle 4x4 market. Yet again, the experiment has paid dividends, such that the Discovery has emulated the Land Rover by running to three generations. Finally, in terms of the stars of the story, there is the Freelander, unveiled in 1997 to compete with smaller rivals.

There has also been a long-running connection between Land Rover and the Army, not to mention various police forces and fire brigades and a chapter examines this link in detail.

Over and above these uniformed Land Rovers, there have also been a plethora of special vehicles down through the years. Some of these have proved long-standing, some short-lived, but another chapter looks at the most interesting of these specials.

Chapter 2

History of Rover

RIGHT An early Rover at the 1905 Olympia Motor Show

IT WAS THE LEAST LIKELY OF beginnings for Rover when James Starley and Josiah Turner founded the Coventry Sewing Machine Company in 1861. However, Starley was also known as "the father of the safety cycle" and was forever looking at ways of reducing risk in cycling – the company began making bicycles in 1869. There was some crossover with the company of Sutton and Starley that was formed in 1878 under the management of John Kemp Starley, his nephew, with William Sutton. The company introduced the first Rover tricycle to the production line in 1883, and the Rover Safety Bicycle in 1885.

In 1888, the Rover Electric Carriage was developed, known as Coventry's first car, although it was more of an electric tricycle. The following year, Sutton departed and the company became JK Starley and Co. Still, the main brand name was gradually taking over and the Rover Cycle Company began in 1894. Even though Starley died in 1901, the experimentation continued and 1903 saw the first of its Motor Cycles coming onto the market.

The company's first recognisable car started to be developed in 1904 by Edmund Lewis and in 1906 it was launched successfully as an eight-horsepower single-cylinder vehicle. That same year, cycle production ceased and the name was changed to the Rover Car Company. A major publicity coup followed when the Rover 16/20hp model beat all its rivals by over 12 minutes in the 1907 Isle of Man TT Race, giving it a kudos that lasted until 1914.

After the First World War, the company resumed operations and in the

1920s the Rover Eight and Rover Ten were steady sellers. There was another public relations bonanza when the Rover Light Six beat Le Train Bleu in a race across France from St Raphael to Calais in 1930.

However, the company was saddled with too many vehicle lines and struggled into the 1930s, making far more cars than it was able to sell. Total collapse was looming when Spencer Wilks arrived, soon took over as managing director, and – supported by his brother Maurice – set about reorganising the Rover product lists, ensuring high quality at all times. The move was successful and the company survived, going swiftly back into profit. Among the 1934 models that helped to revive the company's fortunes were a new 1.4-litre Ten, a four-cylinder Twelve, a 1.6-litre Fourteen and a 16hp Meteor Saloon.

From 1937 to 1945, the company gave over its factories at Acocks Green and Solihull to the war effort, building aircraft engines. Unfortunately, the New Meteor Factory in Coventry was badly bombed and was never

to recover. The Luftwaffe had made sure that Rover was going to become a Birmingham-based rather than a Coventry-based operation.

Consequently, Spencer and Maurice Wilks switched all production to Solihull after the war and, fired by the runaway success of the Land Rover, were again able to revive the company's fortunes. Their stewardship ensured that Rover remained a force in the industry throughout the 1950s and early 1960s.

As well as the Land Rover, the company once more had a roster of well-made, high quality private vehicles that gave it an excellent reputation; the Rover 80, the P5 and the P6 amongst them. Perhaps this was its golden age.

The company bought its fellow Coventry motor concern, Alvis, in 1965, but it proved to be its swansong as a private organisation. The industry was changing out of all recognition and Rover itself was acquired by Leyland in 1966 and merged with Standard Triumph into the truck company's car division.

That state of affairs didn't last very long. Leyland merged with the British Motor Corporation to form British Leyland in 1968 with Donald Stokes as its chairman and so began a most difficult time for the Rover marque. Industrial action and mismanagement were rife at the time and the newly-formed corporation was soon out of money. The government bailed out British Leyland in the early 1970s when Stokes appealed for support, but the price was that this action effectively nationalised the company. Rover cars did not receive sufficient investment – only the established values of Land Rover and Range Rover kept the name to the fore.

Michael Edwardes's much publicised flirtation with Honda kept the pot bubbling until, in the middle of the 1980s, things took a turn for the better. Graham Day became chairman, renamed the company the Rover Group and shifted products upmarket in an echo of the earlier move made by Wilks.

Part of his brief was to find a buyer if he could, and this strategy worked. He managed to sell the business to British Aerospace in 1988, which meant that Rover was now re-privatised. However, the new owners were not themselves car manufacturers and there was a sense that their overlord-

LEFT Chairman, Michael Edwardes outside Leyland's London Piccadilly offices

ship (which by the terms of the sale had to last for a minimum of five years) was merely an interregnum.

So it proved. The German company BMW was anxious to buy Land Rover but were informed that the business was not for sale in pieces. Thus BMW acquired the Rover Group in 1994 and promptly brought their attributes of research, development and planned investment to the company.

At the turn of the millennium, BMW decided to capitalise on its Rover assets. The Phoenix Consortium bought the manufacturing plant at Longbridge and renamed the company MG Rover. The factory at Cowley in Oxford was retained by BMW for building the new Minis. Meanwhile, the Land Rover share of the business was sold to the Ford Motor Company in the spring of 2000.

For the first time, Rover and Land Rover had become separate entities. It didn't last. The Phoenix Consortium went bust in 2005, sold the Longbridge assets of MG Rover to the Nanjing Automobile Group of China, which, in turn, had to allow BMW to sell the Rover name (for a mere £6 million) to Ford, exercising its option of first refusal to buy the brand rights.

LEFT The new Mini Cooper manufactured by BMW Motors

Chapter 3

Spencer &
Maurice Wilks

SPENCER BERNAU WILKS, THE ELDER of the two brothers, trained as a barrister but was joint managing director of Hillman until they were bought by Rootes Bros and he joined many of the people working there in an exodus. He took over as general manager at Rover in 1929.

His prompt action saved the company from oblivion. In 1931, when he took over as managing director, its popular range ran from the Ten at £189 to the prestigious 2.6-litre Meteor, priced at £398. But there were just too many lines – and not enough were selling.

Wilks offloaded the old Meteor Works the following year and concentrated production on the New Meteor Works in Helen Street, Coventry. Soon, after several years of losses, Rover was back in profit.

In 1933, he refocused production on the upper end of the market, a tradition that was to be maintained for several decades. His rationalisation had also reestablished the company's reputation for cars that were a cut above the competition. After a successful 1937 revamp of its range, the company joined the government's "shadow factory" scheme for war production in 1938. At the end of the Second World War, however, production of all Rover vehicles was moved to Solihull, following the sale of the bombed New Meteor Works in 1945.

Maurice Cary Wilks, unlike his elder

brother, wanted to be an engineer from the beginning. He trained in the USA with General Motors from 1926 to 1928. When he returned to England, he joined Spencer at Hillman as planning engineer. During the upheaval, he similarly resigned and followed his brother to Rover in 1929. He duly became chief engineer in 1931 and can take a large share of the responsibility for putting into practice the plans for a rationalised product list.

During the war he applied himself most to aircraft engine production,

helping Frank Whittle to develop the gas turbine engine (despite Whittle being initially less than chuffed with Rover's involvement). Partly as a result of his successful work on the Land Rover, he was made a director of the company in 1950. He became joint managing director with his brother in 1956 and took over as sole managing director in 1961, when Spencer became chairman.

Maurice took over as chairman in 1962 when Spencer retired from the business, but he died in Anglesey the following year, aged 59.

Chapter 4

Series I

RIGHT Land Rover
Series I 1957

AFTER THE SECOND WORLD WAR, Rover found itself with a vast empty factory at Solihull on the outskirts of Birmingham that peace had freed from the pressing requirements of aircraft engine production. This space needed to be put to profitable use. Spencer Wilks, assisted by his brother Maurice, put forward some ambitious plans for mass production of high quality family cars, which would re-establish Rover's market position of the late 1930s. The Ministry rejected the plans because they would use up too many vital resources.

The hunt was therefore on for a new model that would have low investment costs, quickly find a market, be simple to design and produce, and, because of the steel shortage at the time, could use aluminium panelling in its construction.

Legend has it that by 1947 Maurice Wilks decided he needed to replace the ex-US Army Jeep he was using to get around his farm on Anglesey in North Wales. At the time, the only possibility was to buy another Jeep – but Maurice thought several improvements could be made. Being the chief engineer for Rover this problem stimulated his brain cells and he came up with a solution that offered the first commercial 4x4 off-road vehicle, although no-one would have used quite those words at the time (except to escape private car purchase tax, of course).

Maurice's intention, transmitted to his main acolytes, Robert Boyle, Tom Barton, Gordon Bashford and Olaf Poppe, was to provide a vehicle that would be useful to a farmer in every task he had to undertake. In other words, the Land Rover had to be able to pull carts and equipment, transport sheep

and carry straw bales. It also had to have power take-offs, and plenty of bolt-on accessories such as winches.

In those days of shortage and necessity after the Second World War, design and testing did not take so long as they do now. Maurice and his team worked fast, freely admitting that they based their design very closely on the Jeep. The Land Rover was first officially unveiled at the Amsterdam Motor Show on 30 April 1948. The price for the basic model was fixed at £450.

However, assembly lines were still being prepared, and the initial deliveries were not made until July. Except for the first few vehicles (all grey-green) the early models were all painted cockpit green, as had been used for the Avro Anson aeroplane.

Originally, it was primarily intended for agricultural use although it soon took on military connotations (the British Army soon took to it and had adopted it as its standard vehicle of choice by 1956). Take-up by farmers was even more rapid; soon no self-respecting farm could be without one.

But the range of buyers rapidly exceeded expectations. Crucially, the reigning monarch, George VI, bought one for use at Sandringham and Balmoral. The wartime Prime Minister, Winston Churchill, acquired one for his estate at Chartwell while foresters and the police were also keen. Moreover the marque attracted many overseas customers, especially in Africa, many parts of which were then still under British rule.

This suited the ministers in the Labour government, needing exports to offset the UK's massive war debts, who were keen that the Land Rover should be consciously created with the aim of serving the export market. To those ends, much publicity concentrated on how adaptable it was in coping with various off-road environments – not just countryside, hills and mountains,

NXN1

but jungles, deserts and all types in between. And, as a result, planned production in the first year was hugely increased from 1,000 to 8,000.

The prototype of the Land Rover had no fixed roof, but there was a soft canvas top that could be fitted. Seating in the cabin was three abreast, either in seats, or across a padded bench. The standard model was a two-door truck-cab pickup on a box-section steel ladder chassis. This chassis was painted silver at first before that was also changed to green.

There was no doubt that it was a boneshaker, built for utility not comfort, and Land Rover was very proud of this fact, since it ensured that drivers didn't try to push them too hard and ask the admittedly tough systems to absorb too many shocks. It was a working vehicle, with the potential to go anywhere and do anything. It wasn't designed to be a speed king.

Later in 1948, the first of many special vehicles was produced: the Station Wagon. This came in either three-door or five-door versions, and was a seven-seater. This prototype did not prove as popular as it was later to become, and the original version was decommissioned in 1951. A significant part of

the reason was the cost – at a price of £949, it was an expensive vehicle for the era, and was classified as a private not a commercial car. The company went back to the drawing board and later rectified its mistake.

The first engines used were 1.6-litre (1,595cc, to be accurate) taken from the Rover P3 passenger car but there was a distinct feeling that these were sometimes a little underpowered at low revs for the tasks that the vehicles had to perform. In fact, maximum power on these early models was only 50bhp at 4,000rpm and maximum torque was 80lb ft at 2,000rpm, a far cry from what they were later to become.

By 1951, the engineers, responding to demand, had installed a 2.0-litre engine (1,997cc) which became standard for all subsequent models, with the exception of the diesel engines that were introduced as an alternative in the last year of production, from 1957 to 1958. Their capacity was 2,052cc.

The 2.0-litre petrol engines increased maximum power marginally to 52bhp at 4,000rpm and maximum torque to 101lb ft at 1,500rpm. Experience had proved that the vehicle was prized for its capability of grinding over difficult

LEFT The Duke of Edinburgh at the wheel of a 1955 Land Rover

terrain at low revs, so it was the peak torque that needed most attention. For the diesel engine comparative figures were 51bhp at 3,500rpm and 87lb ft at 2,000rpm. All models used a four-speed manual gearbox with syncromesh on top and third gears, and until 1950, when a rear-wheel drive option was introduced, were all four-wheel drive. Top speed for the later 2.0-litre models was 59.5mph (95.7kph). These could accelerate from 0-50mph in 24.9 seconds. Average fuel consumption was 21mpg (or 13.5 litres for every 100 kilometres).

The price of the early models soon rose. Because so many of the features which we would regard as basic were sold as extras (such as seats for passengers, the canvas roof, doors, a spare wheel), the on-the-road price often came to considerably more than £450. This aroused considerable discontent. Six months after launch, the company hierarchy bit the bullet, added in the extras as standard, and raised the price to £540.

Perhaps the most crucial changes were those that affected the wheelbase. In the 10 years of its life, from 1948 to 1958, the Series I Land Rover (as it was subsequently called when the Series II model came to be launched) had

five distinct wheelbase sizes.

From 1948 to 1954, the wheelbase on all models was 80 inches (2,032mm). Fundamentally, the load-carrying capacity was not that large, and customer demand made an upgrade worthwhile. What Rover had found was that farmers didn't need the Land Rover to echo the properties of a tractor, because they invariably had tractors of their own. They needed carrying capability and versatility. Throughout 1953, engineers were testing increases for this version – while at the same time they were also planning to provide a considerably bigger model.

From 1954 to 1956, the standard wheelbase became 86 inches (2,184mm) and in 1955, a longer wheelbase version of 107 inches (2,717mm) was produced, which lasted until 1958. Finally, in 1957, the smaller wheelbase size was upgraded to 88 inches (2,235mm) and, in the following year, the larger model was expanded to 109 inches (2,769mm).

However, the look of the Land Rover changed very little throughout this period, although various bodyshell tweaks were made. Competition in most parts of the world was non-existent (Jeep mainly confined its

activities to the USA) so the relatively slow-moving pace of change was understandable, especially when financial constrictions on development were taken into account. Nevertheless, something had to be done eventually.

For a model that was originally envisaged as a temporary stopgap to utilise production space, sales of Land Rover had shattered all preconceptions. The last examples of the 218,000 Series I models were produced in April 1958, and in September of that year, the very last 107 Station Wagons were produced (a more economic version had been reintroduced in 1954). By that time, the next phase in Land Rover's evolution was ready.

Chapter 5

Series II

BY THE LATE 1950S, THE LAND Rover was firmly established and the company management could indulge in the luxury of fine tuning its success story at leisure. Or so they thought. Apart from the Jeep, whose new output was on the whole confined to the USA, there was no real competition, they believed – until the British Motor Corporation started headhunting Land Rover engineers to help design their planned rival, the Austin Gipsy.

This alerted the powers at Rover who responded swiftly and the Series II was launched at the Amsterdam Motor Show in April 1958, 10 years after the unveiling of the first Land Rover. It was still ahead of the game.

The company had recently created a Styling Department, run by David Bache, and its refinement of the basic design was essentially to last for the lifespan of the marque. The changes from the original were subtle but they were effective. The Series II was still built on a ladder-style chassis frame with mainly aluminium body styles. That much didn't change.

What the styling department did, within strict budgets, was to add improvements to the starkly functional design of the Series I models in nearly every detail. Instrumentation, seating, doors, panels and skirting were all enhanced, so that the Land Rover moved slightly, almost imperceptibly upmarket. So did the price, naturally – the basic price structure now began at £640, which still represented great value for money.

At least customers thought so, because they continued to buy vehicles in vast quantities. Their choice ranged from an estate car to an open-

ABOVE Long 109, 10
seater 1966

top pick-up, from a van to a truck cab. By November 1959, sales of the Land Rover reached 250,000 and the company were producing 30,000 each year.

The most significant upgrade occurred underneath the bonnet. A much larger, more powerful 2.25-litre engine (2,286cc) replaced the 2.0-litre version that had been used in later Series I models. This had the effect of increasing maximum power on these models to 70bhp at 4,250rpm and buttressing maximum torque to a resilient 120lb ft at 1,500rpm. There was selectable two- or four-wheel drive in high range, and permanent four-wheel drive at low range.

Top speed for the new engine models was now 68mph (109.5kph), and they were able to accelerate from 0-50mph in 16 seconds. However, there was a price to pay for this enhanced performance – fuel economy dropped to 18mpg (or 15.7 litres for every 100 kilometres).

BELOW Land Rover on rails mid 1960s

LEFT Land Rover
Cuthbertson Tracked
1965

All models used a four-speed manual gearbox with syncromesh on top and third gears, and with reverse.

Right from the start, the new version came in two wheelbase sizes: 88 inches and 109 inches. These were exactly the same as those which had graced the latter day Series I vehicles, showing that customers felt the engineers had essentially got this right.

Over 110,000 Series II models were produced between 1958 and late 1961/ early 1962, but the Rover management decided not to rest on their laurels. In 1962, a further refinement to the marque was introduced in the shape of the Series IIA. It might not superficially have seemed greatly different, but Land Rover was following its general management credo of changing a little at a time so that models were gradually upgraded without alienating loyal customers.

Essentially, the more rounded lines of the Series II continued to feature on the IIA, so there was no change in basic design, but what continued to proliferate were the different types and special derivatives that poured forth from Solihull. As an example, a 12-seater version of the estate car (Station

Wagon) was launched as an alternative to the standard 10-seater. What's more, it cost almost £350 less at £950. Why? The Purchase Tax laws decreed that 12 seats constituted a bus, attracting no tax, whereas having 10 seats was the hallmark of a taxable private vehicle.

Meanwhile, other types were developed for use by the Army and the Forestry Commission, and a special Forward Control model was introduced in 1962, moving the cab forward above the engine, to be upgraded four years later. However, major changes were designated elsewhere.

The main improvements were to the diesel engine option. This was enlarged to the same size as the petrol engine at 2,286cc, leading to increased power at 62bhp at 4,000rpm and seriously increased torque of 103lb ft at 1,800rpm. For the moment, the capacity of the petrol engines remained the same, but engineers were working on an upgrade, which eventually came through.

In 1967, a six-cylinder 2,625cc petrol engine was introduced as an option for the larger wheelbase models. This increased maximum power on these models to 83bhp at 4,500rpm and

cranked up maximum torque to a very sturdy 128lb ft at 1,500rpm. As for the Series II, the existing sizes of 88 inches (2,235mm) and 109 inches (2,769mm) were retained, so well established had they become.

In September 1968, the company brought in a special one tonne version of the 109 inches wheelbase model, the 101 Forward Control. At the same time a lightweight version of the 88 inches version was put on the market.

Apart from these innovations, the design and modifications of the Series IIA stayed relatively static throughout the 1960s, particularly as the company was integrated into the newly-formed British Leyland in the latter part of the decade.

In June 1971, the company celebrated sales of the 750,000th Land Rover, which meant that 532,000 units of the Series II and Series IIA had been sold since their introduction in 1958, well over 420,000 of which were of the Series IIA models. At the height of demand, production had been peaking at way above 50,000 in the late 1960s.

But things couldn't stay the same forever - now it was time for another major change.

LEFT Land Rovers have always been tough and capable

Chapter 6

Series III

AFTER THE TAKEOVER BY LEYland and that company's subsequent merger with the British Motor Corporation, Rover was in an unaccustomed position. Land Rover was one of the few profitable parts of the British Leyland group, but this could not be relied upon indefinitely. Ten years on from the launch of Series IIA, the market had altered drastically. Throughout the 1960s, rivals had gradually been getting their act together and, by the time it came to launch Series III in 1971, there was significant competition from all around the globe.

In the USA, the long-running Jeep had been joined by the International Scout. In Japan, the Nissan Patrol and the Toyota Landcruiser were cutting a dash and in Brazil, the Ford Rural and the Toyota Bandeirante were on stream. Land Rover's ability to maintain its dominant market position was under serious threat, and with other companies planning to enter the fray, things weren't going to get any easier.

However, within the British Leyland group, the Land Rover had at least seen off its internal competitor, the Austin Gipsy, de-listed just at the time when the former's engineers freely admitted that the latter was becoming a decent vehicle. So they were confident that the Series III would not only underline the marque's historic advantages in off-road versatility and strength but that it could also give these late entrants to the niche market a run for their money in sales terms.

The little matter of launching the Range Rover in 1970 had left the war chest relatively empty for developing the Series III. At heart, it was agreed that the look and feel of the Land Rover was still very much as its customers liked it, so there was little incentive for major change. There were, of course, a few external modifications, including a rectangular rather than an oval badge and alterations to the headlamps and radiator grille. Internally, the instrumentation panel was spruced up. But, by and large, on the principle that "if it ain't broke, don't fix it," the styling department left well alone.

Nor were there many initial changes to the engine. Early Series III models mostly had the same engine (2,286cc) as their later Series IIA counterparts, with maximum power of 77bhp at 4,250rpm and a maximum torque of 124lb ft at 2,500rpm. As with Series IIA, the top speed for these engine models was still 68mph (109.5kph), and they were able to accelerate from 0-50mph in 16.8 seconds. Fuel consumption was still pegged to 18mpg (or 15.7 litres for every 100 kilometres).

In order to give more oomph, a six-cylinder petrol engine had been introduced in the last years of IIA, which gave maximum power of 83bhp at 4,500rpm and possessed a maximum torque of 128lb ft at 1,500rpm. This 2.62- litre six-cylinder engine had a top speed of 73mph (116kph) and was able to go from 0-50mph in 17 seconds, but fuel economy was unsurprisingly even lower at 16mpg (17.6 litres per 100 kilometres).

But Series III engines did belatedly receive a boost – the coming of the V8. Buyers of the longer wheelbase models gained an additional choice of having a de-tuned version of the 3,528cc V8 engine from the Range Rover installed. When this modified V8 engine joined the roster in March 1979, its maximum power was 91bhp at 3,500rpm and it was able to produce a massive maximum torque of 166lb ft at 2000rpm (although both were considerably less than that offered by the tuned-up version). The 3.5-litre V8 engine produced a top speed of 76mph (122kph), could

LEFT Land Rover 109 with hydraulic platform 1973

SERIES III

RIGHT The new Series III sported a revised fascia

accelerate from 0-50mph in 16.9 seconds, and would average 17mpg (16.7 litres per 100 kilometres).

The most crucial technological advance was in the transmission; a new four-speed all-synchromesh gearbox was fitted. And in 1974, the facility to include overdrive and increase fuel economy had been added, with perfect timing, given the petrol supply crisis that struck that year.

Yet again, wheelbase sizes remained constant at 88 inches (2,235mm) and 109 inches (2,769mm) – it was only the introduction of a new type of Forward Control One Tonne special vehicle in 1985 with a base of 101 inches which broke the unvarying pattern.

In many other aspects, the Series III models also stayed much the same. Suspension, steering and brake systems were essentially unchanged. This meant that the way a vehicle handled, although improved, was instantly recognisable to anyone who had driven an earlier Land Rover.

By 1980, the price of a Series III pickup with a V8 engine was £7,550, while the station wagon (now attracting VAT, the replacement for Purchase Tax, as a private vehicle) cost £8,600. Land Rover

vehicles had now been on the market for over 30 years and were fast approaching late maturity. The challenge was to prevent them from becoming moribund.

Sales for Land Rover were falling away from their peak – the company celebrated the cumulative production of 1,000,000 vehicles in 1976 with annual output of over 50,000 – throughout the late 1970s, thanks to the twin onslaughts of fierce competition and industrial unrest, and by the 1980s, annual figures were slipping from 51,000 in 1980 to 41,000 the following year, and just over 25,000 in 1984.

Series III models had been on the books for even longer than their predecessors. Management began to scale down production, but before they were phased out entirely, some replacements were already on the stands. Because the company was, for the first time in its life, a separate concern as Land Rover Ltd (albeit still part of a huge unwieldy nationalised industry), this tapering effect, juggling the old and the new was possible. Even if it appeared, to some, confusing.

Land Rover responded with, what was for them, a revolutionary new way of thinking.

Chapter 7

Range Rover

THE IDEA OF A MORE REFINED 4x4 had been mooted as far back as the 1950s but it wasn't until 1970 that the Range Rover made its long-awaited arrival on the motoring scene. As with the Land Rover, it was Maurice Wilks who was the inspiration behind the new offering.

Following the successful introduction of the Series I, coupled with the launch of the P4 saloon, Wilks had made the decision that a vehicle was required to bridge the gap between the two and set his designers to work. Unfortunately, Wilks was not sure about how he wanted to bridge the gap and uncertainty reigned regarding whether to build a two-wheel drive or four-wheel drive car, although he did come up with the name Road Rover. An early prototype was nicknamed the "Greenhouse" because of its large expanse of glass but the project was shelved in 1958 because it had been designed as a two-wheel drive estate car and, as such, was not that much different to models already on offer. If it had offered the same sort of comfort as a road car but with distinctive off-road capabilities, the outcome would have been different…

The Road Rover was discarded as the company concentrated on their new Rover 2000 project, but key personnel still held the belief that a luxury Land Rover was just around the corner. The mid-1960s arrived and people such as designers Gordon Bashford and Spen King began working on ideas that would eventually evolve into the Range Rover. The vehicle needed to be larger, faster and more comfortable than its predecessor, and combine the appeal of the

Land Rover with the successful aspects of the company's cars. It also needed to be able to tow a caravan, horsebox or boat, and enable the occupants to travel in style.

In 1966 the situation became dire for Land Rover with a freeze on wages, dividends and prices, coupled with the British Army's withdrawal from East of Suez that saw orders fall dramatically. A financial crisis soon led to a devaluation of the pound and the company was in dire need of a boost.

The pair decided from the outset that their new offering had to be a four-wheel drive although they thought that the suspension should be softer than that of the Land Rover. Hence the introduction of coil springs rather than the traditional leaf spring system currently in use on their off-roader.

Choice of engine was also paramount, and the final decision came to rest on the Rover 3.5-litre V8 power plant that was so popular at the time for the project that had become known as the 100 inch Station Wagon. The engine, however, proved too powerful for the Land Rover drive train, so modifications had to be made that saw engineer Frank Shaw delegated with the task of creating a centre differential that allowed the front and rear axles to run at different speeds. The previous moniker of Road Rover would later be adopted before a final settlement on the now familiar Range Rover.

The end of 1966 saw the beginning of the construction of the prototype and many of the features were innovative to say the least. The car was permanent four-wheel drive, a new four-speed all-syncromesh gearbox was installed, as were disc brakes all-round and the suspension was set up so that the wheels would be in contact at all times with whatever terrain the vehicle was traversing. King and Bashford had seen a self-levelling strut in a Mercedes Benz at a recent motor show and utilised the technology in their creation. In a move that was before its time, power steering was going to be offered as an optional extra.

The body styling saw a chunky two-door station wagon leave the drawing boards, with a split tailgate that ensured easy access. The front seat-belts were anchored to the seats rather than to the body so that it was easier to enter and exit the rear seats. But there were further complications on

the horizon as Rover had become part of British Leyland in early 1967 and it was down to the new owners to decide whether this new project would come to fruition or not. Luckily for those involved in the concept, the management backed the decision to fill a gap in the market and actively pushed for an earlier completion date.

Design features – such as a petrol cap hidden behind a flap, internally-hinged doors and a plastic interior that could be hosed down as necessary – were quickly agreed upon, and it was anticipated that production would start in 1969. Initial plans were drawn up to enter a team driving Range Rovers in the London-Mexico World Cup Rally due to take place in April 1970. This proved impossible so a team of Austin Maxis were sent instead – this was not such a disaster as the recently-launched Maxi was the first British production car to feature a five-speed gearbox, something that has become commonplace in today's cars.

One of the main hindrances to the Range Rover's progress was the lack of shared components with any other of the company's range of vehicles. Sure,

LEFT Range Rover V8
3.9 1993

LEFT Range Rover V8
3.9 1993

RANGE ROVER

RIGHT Range Rover
4.0 1997

the V8 engine was already in production but it did not have any parts similar to its cousin the Land Rover, and British Leyland were keen to push the Morris Marina and Triumph Stag. Despite being launched in June 1970, only 86 Range Rovers were produced in the next two months while the next 12 months saw a slightly better total of around 2,500. This was not enough to keep up with demand, however, and British Leyland found themselves in danger of losing potential customers to their rivals.

The Range Rover found a perfect niche and became the first of the commuter's 4x4s. It seemed that everyone was desperate to own one of the luxurious off-roaders although some were put off by the 15mpg consumption figures. Still, it was seen as a status symbol to own one and the rich and famous soon flocked to the showrooms in their thousands.

The Range Rover soon became the car to be seen in and was soon purchased by organisations such as the police and other such institutions and rapidly became a mainstay on British roads. Such was the clamour for Range Rovers that second hand models were

soon selling for ridiculous prices as demand outstripped supply.

January 1973 saw the inclusion of previously optional extras as standard features while the cost of the Range Rover spiralled during that

decade according to official figures. The range was again upgraded in the mid-1970s with a non-slip mat being fitted to the boot while overdrive was offered in 1978. Indeed, the price hardly seems to have stopped rising; the origi-nal entry price in 1970 was £1,998 while a top of the range vehicle costs around £85,000 in today's market.

More than a decade after the marque's arrival saw the introduction of a four-door model in 1981 following an

increase in demand. Numerous companies such as Rapport, Carmichaels (who also produced a LWB three axle model) and Wood and Pickett were already offering conversions that doubled the number of available doors. The following year saw the introduction of automatic gearboxes.

Further specials were offered following the use of a Range Rover in *Vogue* magazine's Lancôme and Jaeger collection photo shoot in Biarritz. While 1,000 special editions were released, the Vogue name has come to symbolize the top of the range Range Rover.

By 1985, the number of two-door models sold had dramatically decreased so that option was discontinued. The same year saw modifications introduced that included a fuel injected engine and advances that further distanced the Range Rover from the Land Rover, while the following year saw the marque join the diesel revolution.

Further improvements were introduced over the years until the evolution of the Range Rover took a dramatic twist in 1994. The original concept had been in production for more than 20 years but found itself fronting more rounded features in keeping with the mid-1990s. A new chassis, revamped engines and air suspension were integral components of the second generation Range Rover as new owners, BMW, looked to take the perennial favourite into the 21st century. Even more modifications were introduced as the millennium drew to a close but 2001 saw a big change.

The third generation of the Range Rover brought the car firmly into the 21st century with a modern design and all the added extras that could be expected of a luxury car. A Sport version was introduced in 2005 with a choice of 4.4-litre V8, 4.2-litre supercharged V8 or 2.7-litre V6 diesel for those who couldn't fight the need for speed. The fourth and latest generation of Range Rover is the best at what it does; it is a fantastic high-end sport utility vehicle that includes both superlative on and off-road driving and today Land Rover cars are better than ever.

The core styling DNA of the Range Rover has been retained with this latest 2013 model, although it does have

LEFT Range Rover Vogue 2003

a lot in common with the existing Range Rover Sport (that has been surprisingly successful). Having said that, the graceful lines and strong poise of the car have never looked better. Size has increased over the third generation Range Rover marginally (a few inches), but interior room has also been rather impressively increased. The fourth generation Range Rover is also a lot lighter. According to Land Rover it is 700 pounds lighter than its predecessor. This has been made possible because most of the Range Rover is now aluminium; that goes for the frame and most of the body panels. Stronger and lighter, the Range Rover is still a heavy car nearing three tons, yet it doesn't drive like one.

The best new features of the 2013

ABOVE Range Rover Autobiography

Range Rover, however, relate to how it drives. It handles so much more like a smaller and lighter car. This is thanks to a combination of systems working in harmony. Land Rover calls the main system Active Dynamics, and it works beautifully in the Range Rover. Techno-controlled stability control, suspension, brake, wheel, and engine systems work together in real-time to make the Range Rover fast and nimble. Roll is greatly reduced, while braking is surprisingly quick. While the Range Rover isn't the first automobile to feature such systems, they seemingly have never felt better in a car meant for going off-road. The dynamic nature of the Range Rover is still its most valuable asset.

The true sport utility vehicle is first

and foremost an all-terrain cruiser meant to travel where roads don't go. Most of today's higher-priced SUVs will roll with grace along motorways, but cough uncomfortably when asked to tread across mud and rocks. Land Rover's entire philosophy is to be good at both, which is reflected in the newest member of the Range Rover family. The very name Range Rover still depicts a vision of class and luxury that is unlikely to be surpassed in the near future.

Range Rover Vogue

FOR A SEAMLESS APPEARANCE, the Range Rover Vogue's exterior features an imposing front grille as well as body-coloured front bumper, vent blades and door handles. A wide choice of interior colours and exterior paints allows for personalisation and there's also a selection of striking 20, 21 and 22-inch alloy wheels, with 20 inch 5 split spoke wheels as standard.

Inside, the interior is upholstered in Oxford leather. There are pow-ered seats with driver's memory and front and rear seats are heated for additional comfort. The state-of-the-art Meridian* Sound System provides stunning sound quality with 380W. (*Meridian is a registered trademark of Meridian Audio Ltd.)

The All-New Range Rover Vogue has two engine options: the LR-TDV6 3.0 Litre Diesel Engine – 258hp, torque 600Nm, maximum speed 130mph, 0-60mph in 7.4 seconds. The second option is the LR-SDV8 4.4 Litre Diesel Engine - 339hp, torque 700Nm, maximum speed 135mph, 0-60mph in 6.5 seconds.

Range Rover Vogue SE

THE EXTERIOR OF THE VOGUE SE has an imposing front grille as well as body-coloured front bumper, vent blades, and plated upper & lower door handles give a seamless appearance. A wide choice of interior colour way combinations and exterior paints allows for personalisation and there's also a selection of striking alloy wheels, with

20-inch 5-split spoke as standard. Inside the Range Rover Vogue SE there are the finest Semi Aniline leather seats. Front seats have driver and passenger seat memory and front climate seats as standard. The state-of-the-art Meridian* 825 Watt Sound System delivers optimised sound quality for all passengers.

Available for the first time on a Range Rover, there's a diesel hybrid powertrain, which achieves improved fuel economy with significantly reduced CO2 emissions. The All-New Range Rover Vogue SE has the same engine options as the Range Rover Vogue as stated above.

ABOVE Range Rover Autobiography

RANGE ROVER

LEFT Range Rover
Sport 2004

Chapter 8

Defender

AS PRODUCTION OF THE SERIES III models began to wind down in the early 1980s, Land Rover management was faced with a dilemma: what could they do to keep sales ticking over, at what was admittedly a difficult time?

The answer was to continue to upgrade the size of the wheelbase and the engines, while at last adding a sense of smoothness to the ride quality, turning on its head the long-held notion that Land Rovers required a bumpy ride to keep them honest.

Although it was the smaller of the two vehicles, the Ninety actually emerged second, in 1984. The reason for this was that there was some to-ing and fro-ing over the size of the wheelbase, which was originally intended to be 100 inches, the same

as that for a Range Rover. Eventually it was decreed that this was too large a jump from the previous 88-inch model, and a compromise was settled upon whereby the dimensions were fixed at 92.9 inches (2,360mm) even though the generic name would be the Ninety. The great advance was the addition of coil springs which guaranteed a far smoother ride.

The first models were only available with the old 2,286cc petrol or diesel engines, but by the following year the V8-cylinder petrol engines had been introduced and, very soon thereafter, the petrol and diesel engines were upgraded to 2,495cc. Maximum power jumped as a consequence to 83bhp at 4,000rpm and maximum torque to 133lb ft at 2,000rpm.

The One Ten came out in 1983, the earlier arrival partly caused by the tweaking to its wheelbase size being more modest – from 109 inches to the nominally accurate 110 inches (2,794mm). As with the Ninety, the addition of coil springs guaranteed a far smoother ride.

Engine power was the other significant development – the One Ten was launched with a variety of options.

The 3,528cc V8-cylinder petrol engine delivered maximum power of 114bhp at 4,000rpm, and a mighty maximum torque of 185lb ft at 2,500rpm. It was also possible to have the 2,286cc petrol or diesel engine fitted. After a year in diesel's case (two in that for petrol) these were upgraded to 2,495cc which marginally increased peak power and definitely heightened peak torque. A modified version of the five-speed gearbox used for Rover and Jaguar saloons and Triumph sports cars was also installed.

Despite these boosts, sales for the Ninety and One Ten fell away gradually throughout the late 1980s (they were 20,686 in 1987, notwithstanding the introduction of a turbo-charged diesel engine the previous year). The sale of the Rover Group business to British Aerospace gave the management time to look again at how they could bring about an upsurge in sales.

The long-running project which resulted in the launch of the Discovery meant that there was a new name on the roster – and the need to redefine what the original Land Rover marque stood for. Its own product listing was in danger of becoming cluttered.

LEFT Land Rover Defender 1993

DEFENDER

Furthermore, the management thinking was that a more evocative name (such as the Discovery, for instance) might generate some excitement.

The main target audience was exactly the same as it always was – people who needed a versatile off-road vehicle – but the whole package of expectations was being dragged slowly but surely upmarket.

There weren't many changes at first, to be frank. The wheelbase sizes remained exactly the same as for the Ninety and the One Ten. There was the usual variety of body shell choices. Coil springs were now a necessity, as were five-speed gearboxes with synchromesh on all gears. The thrills were due to burst from the engine.

The first engines used were the well-established 2,495cc petrol and diesel engines that had served the Defender's predecessors. In fact, maximum power on the diesel models was only 67bhp at 4,000rpm and maximum torque was 114lb ft at 1,800rpm. So far, so ordinary.

But soon engineers had installed a 2,495cc Tdi diesel engine which increased maximum power to 107bhp at 3,800rpm and peak torque to a phenomenal 188lb ft at 1,800rpm. Land

Rover management claimed it also improved fuel economy by 25 percent – quite an overall performance.

By 1994, a 300 Tdi diesel engine had further increased maximum power to 111bhp at 4,000rpm and maximum torque to 195lb ft at 1,800rpm. For the V8-cylinder 3.5-litre petrol engine comparative figures remained as they had done for previous models. A new five-speed transmission, sturdier, smoother and more precise was also brought to market at the same time as the enhanced diesel engine.

At first, sales continued to drop, falling to 16,474 in 1992, but they recovered in the next few years, helped by the improving economic outlook, and had almost doubled to 29,858 in 1996.

In 1998, yet another new engine was installed in the Defender – the Td5 five-cylinder diesel, which was also being used in the second generation Discovery II.

A third wheelbase option (at 130 inches) was also introduced that complemented the 90 and 110. The 2007 (new at tne time) 2.4-litre diesel engine improved the peak torque still further, and the six-speed transmission upped the gearbox ante yet again.

The most current Defender Hard Top,

available in both 90 and 110 wheelbases, offers Defender's supreme functionality with secure load carrying capability.

Defender's 2.2-litre diesel engine produces an impressive 360Nm of torque. With 90 per cent of peak power constantly on tap from as low as 2,200rpm to over 4,350rpm, it provides maximum muscle for tough working environments.

In keeping with the vehicle's iconic status as a truly global product, a

unique engine tune has been developed, which allows it to tolerate the variable quality, high-sulphur fuels to be found across some emerging markets. To cope with the sort of difficult progress that many operations demand, when the engine is working hard at low speed, around 1,000rpm, Land Rover's innovative anti-stall device intelligently adjusts the fuel required to help keep everything running smoothly.

The Defender still continues to sell very well, and very much resembles the classic Land Rover, even though its interior now appears more like that of a car than the piece of farm or military machinery that inspired the original. But what is undeniable is that it still provides the most versatile and powerful off-road vehicle choice, giving greater towing or carrying capability and ability to cope with the most varied types of terrain.

Chapter 9

Discovery

RIGHT The Land
Rover Discovery is as
capable off road as the
Defender

THE TRIUMPHANT SUCCESS OF
the Range Rover had gradually pulled
the 4x4 market ever upward so that
there was now a sizeable gap for
mid-price, mid-range vehicles to fill.
Overseas competitors were pouring
models into this breach, and by the
mid-1980s it became vital for Land
Rover to resuscitate its image and rein-
vent itself as a go-anywhere machine
with a touch of class.

At the same time, the company
didn't want to impinge on the territory of the Defender (then still known
as the Ninety or One Ten), which was
covering the lower end of the market
very nicely. Any newcomer had to
be gauged correctly within their own
product portfolio.

What they really wanted to do was
to attack the Japanese 4x4 models: the
Isuzu Trooper, the Nissan Patrol and,

especially, the Toyota Landcruiser and the Mitsubishi Shogun. A feasibility study began in 1986 to look at cost-effective ways of swiftly developing a vehicle to do this. And if an existing frame could be used in order to slash the costs, so much the better.

It would have been possible to use the framework of either the Ninety or the One Ten, but that would have aligned the new model too closely with the utilitarian sector of the market. The chosen solution was to use the Range Rover chassis, modified with a new body shell and lacking some of the luxury refinements of the older-established vehicle.

By the time that British Aerospace had bought the Rover Group, the recently-privatised management were keen to show that they could use the "Son of Range Rover" principle to deliver a vehicle that was inexpensive to develop and build but was still finely attuned to the needs of the market. The result was the Land Rover Discovery.

The company was very clear that it was designing the Discovery for young urban professionals (the "yuppies", ubiquitous in the late 1980s) who didn't yet have families and didn't expect to do much off-road driving, but wanted to give the impression that they could do so at any stage if they wanted to.

It was a relatively new market, but it was one that newer 4x4 vehicle marques had shown they understood in some measure, providing what the Americans called SUVs (sports utility vehicles). To demonstrate this, Conran Design was brought in to supplement the work of the company's own Styling Department. Consequently, the interior, recognised as very hip at the time, has aged slightly more rapidly than Land Rover's normal, resolutely prosaic style.

The Discovery was launched at the Frankfurt Motor Show on 12 September 1989. The original no-frills price was £15,750, pitched halfway between the cost of a Range Rover and that of a One Ten (the Ninety being a further £1,000 cheaper than its larger wheelbase contemporary).

Originally, when it came on sale in November 1989, the Discovery was only available in a three-door version, to differentiate it from the Range Rover. Strangely, even though the Discovery was like the feisty nephew to the Range Rover's rich uncle, it was also almost six inches taller because of a raised rear-roof panel with extra glass.

Based on a ladder-style chassis frame, it had a steel roof panel and a pressed aluminium shell. There were several lifestyle features, including bull bars, ski racks, electric windows and air-conditioning (although only the V8-engined cars got this initially). All these, and a special trim, ensured the Discovery had a distinctive look.

Naturally it had coil springs, and the face-lifted version of March 1994 had anti-roll bars front and back. At the same time the brakes received ABS anti-lock systems.

The first engines used in 1989 were V8-cylinder petrol (3,528cc to be accu-

rate). Maximum power on these models was a pretty weighty 145bhp at 5,200rpm and maximum torque was also impressive – 192lb ft at 2,800rpm. But Land Rover engineers thought it needed improving. The following year, this was upgraded to a fuel injection V8-cylinder petrol engine (also at 3,528cc), but one capable of summoning maximum power on these models of 164bhp at 4,750rpm and maximum torque of a hefty 212lb ft at 2,600rpm.

Yet again, they didn't stand still. By 1993, the engineers had installed a larger fuel injection V8-cylinder petrol engine (3,947cc) which became standard for all subsequent models, at least for those who didn't opt for diesel. These engines increased maximum power to 182bhp at 4,750rpm and maximum torque to 230lb ft at 3,100rpm.

The same year engineers had installed a smaller four-cylinder petrol engine (1,994cc) which became standard for all subsequent exports to countries where tax breaks favoured engines of less than 2.0 litres. (Seven out of every 10 Discovery cars were being sent overseas, so it made sense.) These engines had maximum power of 134bhp at 6,000rpm and maximum torque of 137lb ft at 2,500rpm.

An obvious alternative was to have a new turbo-diesel engine, and the think-tanks looked at their existing one which had a capacity of 2,495cc. For this diesel engine, comparative figures were 85bhp at 4,000rpm for peak power and 150lb ft at 1,800rpm for peak torque. It wasn't really powerful enough for what was needed – the Discovery was a relatively heavy vehicle.

So the Research & Development team worked on a new Gemini turbo-diesel engine as a more viable option. Yet again, its capacity was 2,495cc. But for this 200Tdi diesel engine comparative figures were a much sturdier 111bhp at 4,000rpm (120bhp with automatic transmission) and 195lb ft at 1,800rpm (221lb ft with automatic transmission). All models used a five-speed manual gearbox with syncromesh on all forward gears, and after 1992, a ZF four-speed automatic transmission option was introduced.

Top speed for the early Discovery models bore comparison with their rivals and, as usual, if drivers really wished to take their vehicles off-road, they could be certain they had the most resilient and versatile models in their

LEFT Land Rover Discovery 1991

class. The wheelbase of the Discovery remained a pretty constant 100 inches (2,540mm), but there were many refinements throughout its career.

In September 1990, Land Rover bowed to the inevitable customer demand, and began to produce five-door Discovery vehicles (perhaps recognising that more and more of their "yuppy" target audience had started families of their own). Fuel injection was brought in to replace a carburetted engine at the same time.

The way the company operated was to provide new technological developments to the Range Rover at first, and then filter them through to the Discovery at the same time as yet further advances were being introduced to the more expensive vehicle – seeking always to maintain a quality gap that justified the difference in price and value.

For this reason, automatic transmission came late to the Discovery as an alternative to the manual gearbox in 1993. For about a year, in fact, the Discovery had exactly the same V8 engine as the Range Rover, tuned the same way, but then the next round of improvements were added to the luxury vehicle in 1994 and the gap

was re-established.

By the end of 1990, over 26,000 Discovery cars had rolled off the Solihull production and assembly lines; annual output was to reach over 50,000 by 1994, nearly 70,000 in 1995 and over 65,000 in 1996. During this heady period, more Discovery vehicles were being made than Defenders and Range Rovers combined. This expansion did, unfortunately, come at the expense of a slight loss of quality control.

In April 1993, the 2.0-litre twin-cam petrol engine became available as an option for the Discovery and, later that year, its V8 engine model was upgraded to 3.9 litres, producing 180bhp.

The BMW takeover of the Rover group from British Aerospace in 1994 was a red-letter day for the marque, because the company immediately launched a well-funded development programme to include research work on the next generation Discovery.

Meanwhile, there was a facelift to the existing Discovery models (after six years, it was due for one), with a new turbo-diesel engine, a new gearbox, plus some cosmetic restyling, the usual host of special editions and a concerted attempt to break into the North

American market, with a particular specification model.

By 1998, the Discovery had been in existence for almost a decade. Almost 400,000 had been built and sold, but the market was shifting faster than ever. Nevertheless, the Discovery had proved that, not only was there a grow-ing niche market, but also that its makers were hip enough to understand it. They were also smart enough to realise that, if they were to flourish, models would have to develop alongside their customers. Once again, as was customary with Land Rover, it was time for a revamp.

Chapter 10

Discovery 2

AFTER BMW TOOK OVER THE business, their management indicated that the previous "make do and mend" approach to product development, which had sometimes characterised Land Rover's progress, was truly at an end. Filled with the confidence of their own success, they ordained a complete overhaul of the Discovery, looking at every aspect to see whether it could be improved.

It had been customary for Land Rover engineers to tinker with their products throughout their shelf life, coming up with a major (or apparent) seismic shift – in their terms – every 10 years or so. The Discovery had been on the books for nine years, so it was ripe for reconstitution. What's more, it was 1998, the year celebrating 50 years since the launch of the first Land Rover, and therefore a publicist's dream.

However, the second generation Discovery was due to be born into a more complex world. The smaller Freelander would come on the market in 1997 and inevitably it would eat into Discovery sales.

The core target audience was slightly redefined as being people in their 40s. Essentially, it was the same group which the Discovery had aimed at, only they had all grown nine or so years older, ceased to be yuppies, and had slightly more mature desires. Even though they might have retained the urge to have a bit of fun.

At first glance, everything looked much the same. Sure, the dimensions had altered a little. It was slightly longer by 7.2 inches (184mm) at 185.2 inches (4,705mm), slightly higher by 2.4 inches (60mm) at 78.0 inches (1980mm) and exactly the same width at 86.2 inches

RIGHT Side view of a
Land Rover Discovery
2003

DISCOVERY 2

RIGHT Land Rover
Discovery TD5 2000

(2,190mm). This had combined to make it possible to fit a third row of forward-facing seats in the tail if necessary rather than the side-facing flip down seats offered in the original series.

But yes, there was the same ladder-style chassis frame, with its steel and aluminium panelling estate car body style and there was the same front engine with four-wheel drive. All the suspension, steering and brake unit features were exactly as for the earlier Discovery. So was the wheelbase which remained constant at 100 inches.

The structure was apparently the same but in reality stronger, because the quality of build had been one of the main bugbears of previous customers. So it might have looked the same – but it was actually different. One example was the door skins which were now made from pressed steel, rather than aluminium. Overall, the Discovery had taken a quantum leap from being a cut-price Range Rover to being very much its own personality.

The original Discovery had used a bewildering variety of engine types, but this time around there really was some change – remarkable stability was shown. There were only two types of engine used with the second generation Discovery; the first was a 2,495cc Td5 five-cylinder diesel engine. This was a considerable step up from the first Discovery's equivalent. In fact, maximum power on these diesel models was 136bhp at 4,200rpm and maximum torque was 221lb ft at 1,950rpm. There was also a 3,947cc petrol engine, which increased maximum power to 182bhp at 4,750rpm and maximum torque to a staggering 250lb ft at 2,600rpm.

Both models used a five-speed manual gearbox with syncromesh on all gears. The ZF automatic transmission was again available as an option. There were ETC (Electronic Traction Control) systems and ACE (Active Cornering

Enhancement) – no one could possibly say that BMW didn't like acronyms.

Needless to say, the two engine types in the new models were both faster and more fuel efficient than any that existed in their predecessor. The Td5, for example, had a top speed of 96mph and average fuel consumption of 26.6mpg.

The new model was showered with awards. In 1999, it received Best Diesel 4x4 (*Diesel Car magazine*), Best Compact Sport Utility (Automobile USA) and Best 4x4 – Highly Commended (Fleet News). The following year it won Best 4x4 off-roader (*Auto Express*) and Best 4x4 (Fleet Management and Business Car), while it walked off with Middleweight 4x4 of the year (*Off Road* and *4 Wheel Drive* magazine) and Best 4x4 (*Auto*

Express) a year later.

Discovery 2 had always been intended as a lever to jemmy open the North American market, and the sales figures tell their own story. In 1997 and 1998, sales in North America were 15,491 and 14,704 respectively, but after a year (1999) when they trod water at 14,230, they jumped to 21,931 in 2000, adjusting downward slightly at 20,860 in 2001. This was a great performance in Jeep's backyard. These sales figures were taken from an overall total of over 50,000 (Discovery 2 was being produced at a rate of over 1,000 per week). Even though the original Discovery had been selling 70,000 vehicles per year at its 1995 peak, this was still a very respectable amount – especially when the advent of the Freelander is also taken into account.

In March 2002, a facelift was given to the Discovery 2 (which only began to be known by this series number at this time), giving its front end the aspect of a third-generation Range Rover. There were many other small improvements and the lucrative North American market was supplied with a new 4.6-litre V8 engine.

By this time, BMW had sold the Land

Rover business to Ford and rumours were already starting to spread that there would not be another 10 years to wait before Discovery 3 could be expected. Just as BMW had been keen to invest in a proven lifestyle vehicle, so now indeed was Ford.

For once, the rumours were spot on. A mere six to seven years spanned the gap between the models – almost unseemly haste in Land Rover lore. Discovery 3 was on its way.

LEFT & ABOVE
Land Rover Discovery
TD5 2000

Chapter 11

Discovery 3

WHEN FORD TOOK OVER THE Rover business from BMW at the turn of the millennium, their management wanted to emulate the previous German owners by showing that they could also develop the Discovery successfully. In order to do so, they needed a model that would expand on the inherent virtues of the marque with a significant range of improvements. Would they be able to achieve this?

Given that Discovery 2 had been introduced to the market in 1998, the Ford hierarchy certainly didn't hang about. The Discovery 3 was launched on November 1 2004.

The core target audience is now quite a wide one – the car has to fit the needs of commercial users, the modern equivalents of squires on their estates, mums on their school runs as well as modern "get up and go" businessmen. In short, it has to be all things to all men.

In that case, it's probably just as well that there are now seven versions for the Discovery 3. The following are available: the Discovery TDV6 5-Seat, the Discovery TDV6 GS, the Discovery XS, the Discovery SE, the Discovery HSE, the Discovery Pursuit LE and the Discovery Commercial. So the Land Rover tradition of building special models for specific markets carries on.

The new model has continued the progress made by the Discovery 2 in offering a more solid build quality – it now seems quite a long way from the jibes about the panelling that were made against the original Discovery. Other safety and security features have also been enhanced. The ABS anti-lock system has been buttressed by the EBA (Electronic Brake Assist) which slams on extra braking power in an

ABOVE Land Rover
Discovery 2004

emergency. There is also a TPMS (Tyre Pressure Monitoring System) which warns against sudden or gradual loss of air pressure.

Comfort is still improving, and Discovery 3 now gives its driver and passengers a ride that is not far short of the luxury afforded to those in a Range Rover. Handling capability has long been a conundrum for the

Discovery engineers to wrestle with, but it seems that the new model has made solid advances in the right direction, leading to a smoother ride. Body roll – a particular criticism of the original Discovery – has been minimised with ARM (Active Roll Mitigation), cornering ability and grip, magnified respectively by DSC (Dynamic Stability Control) and ETC (Electronic Tracking Control) have both been improved and the enhanced four-corner air suspension system no longer gives riders in the vehicle the disorienting feeling that they are drifting. (And if it seems that the new Ford management are as good as the former BMW owners at inventing acronyms to give snappy names to these improvements, that is probably the case.)

All round visibility has always been good because of the commandingly high driving position, but several blind spots have now been eliminated. And it's not just the driver who has a clear panoramic view – so do the passengers. This ability to see clearly is not confined to day time. At night, adaptive Bi-xenon headlamps move left, right, up and down in response to speed, direction, pitch and angle.

There is now an extremely sophisticated terrain response system that reacts to all types of environment, justifying the Discovery 3 in maintaining that it is the leading off-road vehicle in its class. Further backing up that claim, all models are now fitted with a satellite navigation system that works off-road as well as on the roads. Basically there is an on-board Ordnance Survey chart in addition to a road map.

Both exterior and interior styling have been improved. From the outside, the Discovery looks just that fraction better than before, while the inside of the vehicle is packed with more features and better designed than ever.

There are two engines available with the Series 3 – the diesel version is the V6 2,720cc turbo diesel. This represents a considerable advance on previous diesels available. In fact, maximum power on these models is 188bhp at 4,000rpm and maximum torque is an incredible 440Nm at 1,900rpm. The petrol version is a V8 4,394cc, a derivative taken from the Jaguar AJ-V8 4.2 litre. This 4.2-litre petrol engine increases maximum power to 295bhp at 4,000rpm and peak torque has almost risen off the scale. However,

LEFT 2004 Land Rover Discovery V8

observers will not be surprised to learn that such performance comes at a cost in fuel economy.

All models use a six-speed manual or a six-speed adaptive automatic gearbox. The ZF 6HP26 transmission is claimed to be one of the most advanced in the world.

Top speed for the models is listed at 116mph (95.7kph). These can now accelerate from 0-62mph in 11.9 seconds. Average fuel consumption for the diesel is 28mpg (or 9.0 litres for every 100 kilometres). The petrol engine provides, as mentioned, considerably less fuel economy.

As with its predecessor, the Discovery 3 has been deluged with awards. Some of the most prestigious of its 80-strong awards have been Best Large 4x4 (*What Car?* 2005, 2006 and 2007), AXA Car of the Year 2006 and Best 4x4 Off-Roader (*Auto Express* 2005 and 2006).

The Discovery 3 has proven that Land Rover has come a long way from the days when it was first designed as a primarily agricultural vehicle nearly 60 years ago. It is now a thoroughly upmarket vehicle – mind you, at prices ranging from £27,315 through to £44,535, that cachet is reflected in the cost.

Chapter 12

Discovery 4

LAUNCHED IN 2009, THE Discovery 3 was updated significantly, including a larger capacity diesel engine, which culminated in the model name being upgraded to the Discovery 4.

The Discovery 4 looked on the outside like one of the most ingenious interpretations in the automotive industry and the changes that were made mechanically speaking led to the emergence of the Integrated Body Frame – two separate chassis. Both off-road and on-road performance were greatly enhanced. The weight of the Discovery 4, even with a magnesium crash structure up front, still comes in at a pretty hefty 2.5 tonnes, which makes it somewhat of a beast of a car. It should be bore in mind, however, that the car now has an enormous body structure, the individual three-point belts, twin front airbags, full-length curtain side airbags

and optional curtain airbags for the third row – all in all as safe as houses!

In terms of space, Land Rover added just 17.6cm to the length of the Discovery. It may not sound a lot, but this extra means that, what was before a cramped five-seater with two seats for occasional use, was turned into a spacious and comfortable seven-seater with the well-executed foldaway third row now perfectly comfortable for adults.

Revised again in 2011, the 2993cc V6 turbodiesel now produces 251bhp at 4000rpm and 442lb ft at 2000rpm. It is the only engine available in the Discovery and comes with a ZF eight-speed automatic gearbox as standard. Throttle response is good and, vitally, it has much more step-off thrust than the original 2.7-litre car. It has a top speed of 112mph and acceleration speed of

0-60mph in 8.8 seconds. There are just three trim levels for the Discovery 4: GS, XS, and HSE. There is, however, an extensive scope of available specifications and even the entry-level GS includes DAB, Bluetooth and climate control as standard.

Discovery 4 GS

WITH INCREDIBLE POWER AND versatility, the Discovery 4 GS is designed to handle heavy loads and challenging environments with ease. It is both capa-

ble and comfortable, possessing a definitive style, with body coloured wheel arches. Other features include bright halogen headlamps, a Meteor trim finisher to facia and doors and contemporary highlights such as the 4.2-inch colour centre console screen.

The 255hp LR-SDV6 3.0 diesel engine with eight-speed drive select transmission and steering wheel mounted paddle shift uses a sequential mode boosting system to increase the air density entering the engine's cylinders. This enables a correspondingly greater amount of fuel to be injected for increased power output. It also uses the latest materials and sequential turbochargers to optimise responsiveness by delivering increased torque at very low engine revolutions.

Discovery 4 XS

PERFECT FOR EITHER TOWN OR country, the Discovery 4 XS is the smart, practical complement to the modern lifestyle. In addition to its superb drivability, it has the advantage of Land Rover's capability and versatility with electronic air suspension for a constant, level ride height. Sophisticated 19 inch 10 spoke alloy wheels combine with Terrain Response® allowing smooth handling in tough conditions. The engine spec is the same as the Discovery 4 GS as above.

Discovery 4 HSE

THE DISCOVERY 4 HSE IS A PHEnomenal all-rounder: comfort for passengers, versatility for loads and many useful features to make driving easier and more enjoyable. Featuring distinctive fog lamps, the Discovery 4 HSE also includes cruise control for convenience when motorway driving. An intuitive seven-inch full colour touch-screen that controls Infotainment comes complete with phone integration. The engine spec is the same as the Discovery 4 GS and the Discovery 4 XS as above.

Discovery HSE Luxury

BOTH SMART AND SOPHISTIcated, the Discovery HSE Luxury is elegant in the city and extremely capable in the country. With its luxury Windsor leather in distinctive colours, the Discovery 4 HSE Luxury goes the distance in style and comfort. Straightgrained walnut finishers define the elegance of the interior. An impressive array of internal technology includes a seven-inch full colour centre console touch-screen for controlling key vehicle functions, to front and rear parking aids and phone integration. In the Discovery 4 HSE Luxury, every journey is a pleasure. The engine spec is the same as the Discovery 4 GS, the Discovery 4 XS and the Discovery 4 HSE as above.

LEFT Discovery 4 AME

Chapter 13

Evoque

THE FIRST TEN YEARS OF THE 21ST Century will be remembered in motoring circles as an age when manufacturers worldwide strove to build vehicles to meet stringent new rules set down by government bodies. Legislation proclaimed that the average level of carbon dioxide emissions across a manufacturer's catalogue should come within certain limits. Companies historically renowned for building high powered, high fuel consuming cars determined to continue those traditions were forced to reconsider future factory output and include cleaner and greener models to balance any shortfalls.

In January 2008, Land Rover showcased a stunning concept car at the North American International Auto Show, Detroit, hinting at the next generation Range Rover. Designed by Gerry McGovern, the LRX's most notable idiosyncrasy was the rearward tapered roofline, yet maintained a distinct Range Rover family resemblance. It was also particularly small in comparison to other models and when favourable public response prompted the company to enter into full production, it was afforded with a compact crossover SUV to rival the likes of the Nissan Juke and Volkswagen Touareg.

After a three-year gestation period and with the help of a £27 million grant from the British government, assembly got under way in July 2011 at Land Rover's Halewood plant, providing a thousand new jobs for people in and around Liverpool.

Aluminium and composite plastics used extensively to clad the relatively unorthodox (for an off-roader) unitary construction body helped to reduce kerb weight, thus increasing fuel effi-

ciency. Available as a five-door or three-door coupé with the option of front only or four-wheel-drive, it was the first car in Range Rover's illustrious 40-year history to feature a four-cylinder engine with the choice of 2 litre petrol, and 2.2 litre 148bhp or 187bhp diesels. Indeed its public unveiling as a fully-fledged production car coincided with the 40th Anniversary celebrations and dignitaries, including those from the motoring press, invited to the launch party at the Orangery, Kensington Palace were somewhat relieved to see the final form Evoque was almost entirely true to the LRX concept.

With a 'footprint' covering no more road space than a modern family hatchback, the Evoque retained all the comforts of its Range Rover stable mates as well as complimenting the legendary off-road capabilities associated with the marque.

Both the Evoque and Evoque Coupé now have three design levels: the Pure, Pure Tech and the Prestige. The entry level Evoque has a price range starting around £29k. For some years now there has also been interest and speculation as to Land Rover launching a convertible model of the Evoque. At the 2012 Geneva Motor Show the convertible concept was officially unveiled for the first time. At the time of writing, the green light for construction had not yet been given, but watch this space!

Chapter 14

Freelander

WHILE 4X4S HAD BEEN MULTI-plying in numbers since the introduction of the Land Rover Series I in 1948, many other manufacturers had jumped on the bandwagon and by the late 1980s and early 1990s there was a proliferation of choices available. Many had simply offered a four-wheel drive system in their saloons such as Audi (with its Quattro) and Subaru, but it was the increase in popularity of small 4x4s such as the Suzuki Vitara and the Daihatsu Sportrak that prompted Land Rover to come up with the Freelander.

The idea of a "Baby" Land Rover had been mooted since the launch of the Discovery in 1989 and within two years was being taken very seriously. Two separate prototypes were created that would fill the void in the market. Project Oden set about designing a two-wheel drive tall estate car while Pathfinder offered two four-wheel drive versions: a three-door with a removable roof over the rear seating area and a five-door rigid body. While there were distinct similarities in the two fibre-glass-bodied concept vehicles produced in 1993, the Freelander's origins can clearly be seen in the Pathfinder.

It was decided to go with the four-wheel drive suggestion because many city dwellers were buying 4x4s as a status symbol...not because they actually wanted to use the car's off-road capabilities. It was also agreed to take an evolutionary step in the history of Land Rover. All vehicles produced until that point had been built on a separate chassis but the new Land Rover would boast a monocoque bodyshell that had first been introduced into cars in the 1930s and had become almost the norm by the 1960s. Prior to this, most 4x4s – apart

from notably the Lada Riva and the Jeep – had been built with a chassis of sidebars reinforced by cross members to which the body was attached. A further prototype was built under the name of the Cyclone but this bears less resemblance to the eventual Freelander than the Pathfinder.

The project was named CB40 but by January 1994 the company was bought by BMW. The German giant, however, allocated the necessary capital and the real work began. Project director was Dick Elsy, an engineering science graduate of Loughborough University who had been with Land Rover since 1983, and he began putting together a team of experts.

Gerry McGovern was installed as the stylist in charge of the overall design of the vehicle and he quickly set about revising the bodywork so that it didn't give the impression of being a van. A small step was integrated into the roofline of the five-door while the sloping rear window pillar that had been suggested in the Pathfinder concept was reintroduced. In general, the CB40's appearance was made more in tune with the rugged appeal of a tradi-tional Land Rover.

As previously mentioned, it had already been decided that the new vehi-cle should have a monocoque shell but other suggestions included independent suspension – as opposed to beam axles that dictated that one drive wheel would always be on the ground – carried on sub-frames, Hill Descent Control and Electronic Traction Control. These radi-cal ideas did not go down too well with the old guard at Land Rover but were eventually adopted as the performance of the prototypes was exceptional. Such was the reception and success of the monocoque shell, that the third generation of Range Rovers would be revised to incorporate this design feature.

The company undertook in-depth market research and concluded that the three-door model would be aimed at younger customers while the five-door version's target market was families and with both being built to the same sized wheelbase costs could be reduced by being able to share components. Two choices of transversely-mounted engines were initially offered: a 1.8-litre petrol and 2-litre turbo-diesel that had already been developed for insertion into Rover cars but which were relatively easily modified to suit. It was agreed that while most customers would probably rarely use their vehicle off-road, it had to be more than capable in order to avoid damaging Land Rover's reputation.

As all the pieces of the jigsaw came together, the company built more than 200 prototypes. The first 22 saw CB40 running gear – and even interiors – hidden beneath Maestro van body shells. Later models showed more of the even-

tual car's true identity but were kept closely guarded until Land Rover were ready to announce the launch of their new model. That announcement came on 18 March 1997 but it would be another 10 months before the vehicle itself was available for purchase.

By the time the – as now named Freelander – was ready for the public, it did boast a monocoque shell but this had been reinforced by various steel cross members so that the underside of the vehicle did resemble that of a traditional Land Rover. One other distinction between the Freelander and the company's previous offerings was the material used in the construction of the body. While Land Rovers had traditionally used aluminium for their body panels in a throwback to the post-Second World War steel shortages, the Freelander was mainly constructed of steel panels coated in zinc as a rust retardant. In addition, the front wings and wheel arches were manufactured from a composite plastic that supposedly retained its shape after a light impact while the bumpers were colour coded and designed to do the same.

The launch itself was arranged for the

FREELANDER

RIGHT The Freelander
has been a succesful
model in the USA

Frankfurt Motor Show in September 1997 with motoring journalists invited to Andalucia in Spain to test drive the new models for themselves. The schedule had been carefully thought out with the launch at the most important of the mainland European shows…but also the home of German owners BMW. A month later, the Freelander made an appearance at the London Motor Show and generated a surprising 47,000 enquiries that only confirmed the company's belief that the time was right to introduce a smaller 4x4.

The first post-prototype Freelander – number 677 – was decked out in white livery and was signed in felt-tip pen by all the personnel who had been involved in its construction. It was not available for private sale, however, and was presented to the Heritage Motor Centre at Gaydon. The Freelander became the first totally new 4x4 to emerge from the Solihull workshop since 1948.

When it was eventually available to buy from Land Rover showrooms, the starting price for a Freelander was just £15,995 – coincidentally the same as a Discovery had cost on launch in 1989 – and as such was far cheaper than its immediate rivals. In a direct nod to its bigger predecessor, the Freelander was also launched with blacked out window frames, but this was abandoned after around 1,500 vehicles were built because of production problems.

As with the majority of new models, the Freelander suffered mechanical problems during its early years. The most inconvenient faults must have been the steering column locks jamming but other annoyances included loose PAS hoses, poor de-misting, oil leaks and whistling from the heater blowers and central control unit. These niggling faults were quickly solved and 1999 saw the launch of the Freelander Commercial.

It had always been Land Rover's intention to revamp the Freelander before the public became bored with what it could offer and the first stage of this process arrived in 2001. Improvements included the addition of a BMW diesel and a 2.5-litre V6 engine and revised transmissions – including a Steptronic automatic gearbox – along with the introduction of a 400-run limited edition of the Freelander Sport. It was an American specification Freelander that was the three millionth Land Rover to exit the factory and in

a carefully planned publicity stunt this was driven from the assembly line by former Boyzone singer Ronan Keating.

A facelift in 2002 saw all bumpers and exterior plastic mouldings changed from grey to black with additional modifications made to the interior of the vehicles. Further alterations were introduced as the years passed, as Ford – who had bought the Land Rover marque from BMW in 2000 – attempted to stamp its own identity on the brand and continued to do so until the launch of the Freelander 2 in 2006.

Chapter 15

Freelander 2

WITH INCREASED COMPETITION from the likes of Nissan (X-Trail), Toyota (RAV4) and Honda (CR-V), Land Rover and its parent company Ford realised that a revamp of the Freelander was needed and this arrived in 2006 with a debut at the British International Motor Show in London. Its predecessor had become the best-selling off-roader in both Britain and Europe so the company wanted to cement its reputation as the market leader.

One of the main visible differences between the second generation Freelander and the original offering was the disappearance of the spare wheel from the tailgate. The body had been elongated by six inches and the prerequisite spare was now housed under the floor of the boot. The hidden changes included the removal of the monocoque strengthening framework as the overall vehicle was made longer, wider and taller than its forerunner. One disadvantage of this was that its weight had increased but this was offset by the advancement in engine technology over the intervening years.

The new power plants on offer were a 2.2-litre Ford turbo-diesel and a 3.2-litre petrol engine that bore more than a passing resemblance to that utilised by Volvo. It also boasted variable valve timing (VVT), cam-profile switching and an overall sportier response, while the common rail fuel injected diesel was exceptional for its low noise and vibration with its double-walled cylinders.

Other modifications included the raising of vital engine components to prevent flooding while off-roading, and increasing the height of the bonnet in an attempt to protect pedestrians' heads from accidental injury when the

Freelander was being used as a commuting vehicle. Gearboxes on offer were six-speed manual or automatic, depending on which model you were buying, while the latest technology was incorporated into the car with the inclusion of sockets that enabled the driver to connect their i-Pod to the stereo system.

As with most modern cars, a built-in satellite navigation system was available via a touch screen while the onboard

computer warned the user if the tyre pressures were too low. Leg room was also increased for passengers in the rear as Land Rover attempted to corner the small SUV market.

Interestingly, the Freelander 2 – built alongside the Jaguar X-Type at Halewood in Merseyside – was marketed as the LR2 for the North American market while the third generation Discovery was labelled the LR3.

The latest Freelander 2 now encompasses three design levels: the S, the GS and the XS. With the petrol-engine option now a thing of the past, the level-entry S model offers two engine specs: 2.2 litre eD4 Diesel engine with two wheel drive, six-speed manual transmission and intelligent Stop/Start system and the 2.2 litre TD4 Diesel engine with six-speed transmission and intelligent Stop/Start system, both 150hp.

The GS and the XS models offer both of the above engines specs plus two additional automatic options: 2.2 litre TD4 Diesel engine with six-speed automatic transmission with CommandShift® (150hp) and the 2.2 litre SD4 Diesel engine with six-speed automatic transmission with CommandShift® with 190hp.

LEFT The second generation of Freelander was named the LR2 for the American market

Chapter 16

Land Rover
on Duty

RIGHT A Land Rover enters a helicopter in 1956

WHILE THE LAND ROVER MAY have been conceived as an alternative to the Willys Jeep that had proved so successful during the Second World War, it has since gone on to provide invaluable service to both the armed forces and civilian emergency services. The British Army already had plans to develop its own 4x4 because the American Jeeps that were on loan as the hostilities ended would have to be replaced. This vehicle was the FV1800, but production was still a few years in the future so an order for 50 Land Rovers was placed in 1949. Such was the success of the initial batch, that several hundred more were soon purchased.

These 81-inch Land Rovers were fitted with a Rolls-Royce 2.8-litre engine instead of the standard 1.6-litre version. The enhanced power plants delivered 50 percent more power and 75 percent more torque which meant modifying the gear ratios and ended up providing a top speed of 80mph. It wasn't just "simple" things like this modification that were necessary though, as a larger radiator and clutch had to be fitted along with moving the battery to under the passenger seat to accommodate the larger engine in the space available. These Land Rovers faced enemy troops for the first time during the Korean War between 1950 and 1952 and were a successful part of the conflict.

It wasn't long, therefore, before the

Army began placing orders for LWB Land Rovers while the company have created models to serve specific purposes during the intervening years. The Series IIA Lightweight was introduced in 1968 because the standard 88-inch vehicles were too large to be transported side by side in aircraft and too heavy to be safely lifted by helicopters. The first Lightweights saw the headlights fitted either side of the grille which gave them a distinctive look but from 1969 they were moved to a more traditional mounting in the front wings. The Series III arrived in 1972 and stayed in production for another 12 years.

The 109 was the first LWB model that became commonplace in the British Army. The extra carrying capacity of the 1958 introduction soon became valued and it received modifications such as a reinforced cross member, extra front quarter bumpers and twin fuel tanks. More often than not a soft-top, the 109, also underwent several conversions including adding a rigid body to accommodate an ambulance, while several overseas nations requested higher ground clearance, so a drop-shackle suspension was developed.

The 101 Forward Control Land Rover was specifically manufactured for the armed forces to be able to tow 105mm Howitzer guns. Although the work first began on the prototype in 1966, it wasn't until six years later that this model was finally introduced. It eventually went into service in 1975 but production only ran until all orders had been fulfilled three years later. One of the main features of this vehicle was the short overhang of its body at both ends which, coupled with a higher than usual ground clearance, meant that it was exceptional off-road. The 101s were built to a variety of specifications that included both left- and right-hand drive and 12- and 24-volt, but the majority of them were supplied as GS soft-tops although the vehicle did prove a successful base for

an ambulance conversion. Land Rover were unable to produce a road legal version of the 101 so there is no civilian counterpart, although the chassis was taken over by Spanish company MSA once production ceased in 1980 who offered their own take on the design as a Santana 2000.

Other military models that are visually comparable to their civilian cousins include the Ninety and Defender 90, One Ten and Defender 110 and, to a certain extent, the 127 and Defender 130. The introduction of these models in the mid-1980s saw a major change for the armed forces as they opted for diesel engines for the first time. Although diesel-powered Land Rovers had been an option as far back as 1956, most of the vehicles supplied until now had been petrol engined because it was felt that their diesel counterparts were too slow. The 127s were frequently utilised in pairs as Rapier launcher and fire control units. There were versions of the Defender 90, 110 and 130 that had the added moniker of XD (Extra Duty). These were modified to carry bigger payloads, and the XD 130 became the replacement for the dated 101 ambulance in 1997.

LEFT Land Rovers have often seen active service from Northern Ireland to Iraq and Afghanistan

RIGHT A crew prepare
their vehicle for patrol
in Afghanistan

Of course, there have been far too many variants of military Land Rovers over the years for us to be able to include every single one, but one that is worthy of a mention is the Pink Panther. In 1968, the Special Air Service bought 72 long-range desert patrol vehicles built on Series II 109-inch chassis but they were supplied without doors, windscreen and canopy as these were considered unnecessary for desert driving. They were delivered in standard green but many were repainted in pink which was then believed to be the best camouflage paint in the desert. In the Gulf War, their descendants proved invaluable and even outperformed the specially equipped Hummers, but the nickname of "Pinkies" stuck even though they are no longer painted in that colour. The success of these vehicles has led to the development of the rapid-deployment weapons mounts that offer a fixed mounting for machine guns and easy access to allow the soldiers to bring their weapons into action immediately.

Two prototype models that were not taken up by the military were the Llama Forward Control that was proposed to take over from the 101 Forward Control, and the Centaur. The latter boasted a

110 front end while the rear was a shortened version of the Scorpion light tank tracked bogie.

But of course, it is not just the military who have taken advantage of the adaptability of the Land Rover. The police, ambulance and fire services have all used these vehicles to varying degrees. The latter have been employing Land Rovers since the 1950s with Series Is being a more than viable means of getting light firefighting equipment to the scene of a blaze faster than a full-sized fire engine. Series IIA Forward Controls were also popular for small villages while six-wheeled Carmichael TACR2 Range Rovers can be seen at several airports.

Perhaps one of the most awe-inspiring models ever built was the Shorland armoured car that was introduced in 1965 for the Royal Ulster Constabulary in Northern Ireland. Produced by Short Brothers and Harland Ltd in Belfast, it boasted armour plating at a time when the situation in the province was rapidly deteriorating. This vehicle also carried a 7.62mm machine gun and could be equipped with gas or smoke canister dischargers.

LEFT Land Rovers are capable of carrying out a varied range of duties and can be adapted to carry an assortment of weapons and equipment

Chapter 17

Environmental Responsibility

LAND ROVER TAKE THEIR responsibility to the environment very seriously and have an integrated and innovative strategy in place that is called 'Our Planet'. Their plan is simple: to reduce their dependency on fossil fuels and the production of man-made CO_2 emissions, to use fewer resources and create less waste.

This is being achieved by investing in four key areas, areas designed to reduce their carbon footprint, support conservation and humanitarian collaborations and includes one of the world's most comprehensive CO_2 offset programmes.

CO_2 Offset Projects

AS LAND ROVER REACHES ITS 50th CO_2 offset project, the company is celebrating what their whole carbon management programme has achieved over the last six years.

Since 2007, Land Rover has invested in carbon reduction projects across the globe as a means of addressing the environmental impact of their business and their vehicles.

Their first in Uganda is still one of their flagship Gold Standard projects where they delivered 70,000 energy effi-

cient stoves. Made with locally sourced materials and designed to reduce charcoal burnt by 30%, they saved an estimated 200,000 tonnes of emissions by 2011. By using less wood than regular stoves, they also helped reduce deforestation and provide employment in the surrounding area.

Since then, Land Rover has supported a wide range of energy efficient projects around the world. From wind and hydroelectric power to biomass and geothermal energy. These are all designed to reduce emissions, whilst benefiting communities wherever these projects are based. Working with their partners ClimateCare, all their projects are managed to the highest standards of accreditation, such as Gold and Social Carbon Standard to ensure direct community benefits.

Over the last five years, Land Rover investment has improved the health of around one million people with the provision of clean cook stoves. They have also generated more than 2 million MWh of renewable electricity (enough to power London for 21 days). That's in addition to over £30 million worth of investment in sustainable economic growth through creating jobs, sharing technology and reducing carbon dependency.

What's more, they have evolved their approach to use carbon finance to invest in innovative solutions that help improve people's lives. Their 50th project supported the delivery of nearly 900,000 Life Straw water filters to families in rural Kenya. This simple tool safeguards against many of the health risks from contaminated water, such as diarrhoea – Kenya's third leading cause of death, as estimated by the World Health Organisation. By eliminating the need to boil dirty water, Life Straw filters also cut carbon emissions from home fires.

Initially, Land Rover's target was to deliver five million tonnes of carbon reduction in five years. They are proud to say they've exceeded that target – and been awarded a Platinum Corporate Responsibility rating by Business in the Community in the process. They will continue to invest £1.5bn annually for the next five years in new products, R&D and new technologies designed to reduce their overall carbon impact.

E_Terrain Technologies

THE E_TERRAIN TECHNOLOGY is a joint £800m investment into new technologies designed to reduce CO_2 emissions and improve fuel consumption. Land Rover is targeting a 25% reduction in joint fleet average tailpipe CO_2 emissions within the next five years. Beginning with an intelligent Stop/Start system on Freelander 2 TD4 manual in 2009, followed by Intelligent Power Management Systems (IPMS) with Smart regenerative braking on all Discovery & Range Rover vehicles, to the announcement of their new small Range Rover, E_Terrain Technologies form a fundamental part of their overall carbon management plan.

Sustainable Manufacturing

CERTIFIED TO ISO14001 SINCE 1998, Land Rover has world class manufacturing facilities. As a company, they are targeting a 25% reduction in operating CO2 emissions by 2012, 25% in waste to landfill and 10% in water consumption. Going forward they are measuring their total operating carbon footprint and setting targets to reduce it; since 2006 this integrated approach has included the carbon offset of all manufacturing assembly CO2 emissions from their Solihull and Halewood plants. It doesn't stop there, however. Every Land Rover is designed to be 95% recoverable and reusable - with 85% that's recyclable and a further 10% that can be used to generate energy.

Conservation and Humanitarian Projects

FOR OVER 60 YEARS LAND ROVER has worked with conservation and humanitarian organisations around the world. They have five global partners who represent a range of activities, spanning scientific research to preserv-

ing cultural heritage. They are proud to support the critical work of the Born Free Foundation, Royal Geographical Society, Earthwatch Institute, Biosphere Expeditions and the China Research & Exploration Society. More recently, Land Rover launched a new three-year global initiative with the IFRC entitled 'Reaching Vulnerable People around the World' through which Land Rover aims to support IFRC's life saving work.

ABOVE An example of what they are trying to save

Chapter 18

Specialised Models

WHILE LAND ROVERS HAVE starred in many films – particularly of a safari nature – perhaps the most impressive vehicles were the ones created for 1995's *Judge Dredd*. Set in the year 2139, Sylvester Stallone starred as the title character who was charged with keeping law and order in the crime-ridden MegaCity of the future. A total of 31 101 Forward Control models were especially built for the project with the design work being carried out by Gordon Sked and David Woodhouse.

With fibreglass bodies built onto the chassis to emulate a futuristic mode of transport, these were sold after filming had been completed so it is possible to own a 22nd century vehicle. They can easily be adapted to comply with regulations so don't be surprised if you see one looming large in your rearview mirror! You might want to spare some sympathy for the driver though, as noise levels, heat and comfort leave a lot to be desired. The Dunsfold Land Rover Trust and Museum, based in Godalming, boasts one of these in their collection.

A more recognisable Land Rover was created for the 2001 film *Tomb Raider*, starring Angelina Jolie as Lara Croft, with two Defender 110s being adapted at a cost of $175,000 each to enable the intrepid adventurer to triumph against evil. They were open-topped and painted in Bonatti Gray with aluminium tread plates and bumpers, a "Heritage"-type grille and four Safari driving lights mounted on the front of the roof rack. Extra accessories included an expedition tool kit, fender-mounted shovel and axe, winches at the front, rear and sides, a dash-mounted notebook computer, a GPS navigation system, a GSM tel-

ephone and emergency kill buttons.

Following the success of the film, 250 special edition Tomb Raider Defenders were built and sold to the public. They were not, however, exact replicas of the movie vehicles as they were hard-top versions and were powered by a five-cylinder diesel engine rather than the V8 petrol.

There have been many conversions over the years but one of the strangest looking vehicles must have been those created by Cuthbertson and Sons in Biggar, Scotland. Intended for use on marshy terrain, these conversions worked very well on soft ground but the vehicles did have problems climbing banks. A LWB Series II was chosen as the basis for the conversion, then the wheels were removed and a sub-chassis dropped in complete with bogeys and tracks. The steering mechanism was modified at the front end, although it was a totally different experience to its wheeled cousins, and selectable four-wheel drive was also retained.

As Land Rovers became more widely used and the number of expeditions undertaken – both individually and in organised groups – increased, it was no surprise that companies began adapting these versatile vehicles to include sleeping accommodation. Dormobile used the Land Rover to cash in on the camping boom in the 1950s and 1960s with a conversion that gave the vehicles an elevating roof, as well as sleeping and cooking areas. Another company to add sleeping facilities to Land Rover 109s and Range Rovers was Carawagon International who offered a slightly

more strange-looking roofline when erected than the Dormobiles in that they looked rather like a semi-circular coffin anchored to the roof.

For visiting dignitaries, there was a version named the State Review Vehicle which saw the front row of seats retained, albeit without any protection for the driver from the elements. The rear of the Land Rover, however, was heavily modified to offer a raised platform surrounded by a screen so that the occupants could clearly see and be seen but were offered a modicum of protection if necessary.

One of the most bizarre sights, though, must be the amphibian Land Rover. With outriggers attached to either side of the body, buoyancy is achieved courtesy of inflatable airbags while the vehicle is powered through the water by a propeller mounted between the rear differential and the propshaft.

Chapter 19

The Expedition Trail

RIGHT To participate in the Camel Trophy the vehicles had to be heavily modified

LONG BEFORE OTHER CAR MANU-facturers recognised the benefits of taking part in overseas events for publicity purposes, Land Rover were sponsoring organised expeditions. These didn't just spread the fame of the marque, but they also proved invaluable in terms of feedback from the drivers as to how the vehicles had performed in inhospitable terrain.

It was in 1955 that the company first lent two 86-inch Land Rovers to a group of Oxford and Cambridge graduates for their Far Eastern Expedition. The intrepid explorers became the first to drive across country to Singapore, a feat that had never before been accomplished due to the harsh conditions in the jungles of Burma and Thailand. Along the way, the graduates conducted research and the expedition was partially funded by the Royal Geographic Society. Such was the success of this foray into the unknown, that Land Rover participated in future university adventures.

They also provided a pair of Range Rovers for an expedition in the early 1970s to demonstrate the need for a road to be built between North and South America. The Darien Gap was largely swamp and jungle that was impassable for normal vehicles and it was reasoned that a pan-American highway would help developing countries in their efforts to establish better trade links with their neighbours. Land Rover supplied the newly-launched Range Rovers to publicise that their latest model was not just a luxury car but that it could also handle whatever obstacles it might encounter.

As it turned out, the trek was extended from the planned short journey between

North and South America and became a marathon drive from Anchorage (Alaska) to Cape Horn in Tierra del Fuego. The 18,000-mile trip commenced in December 1971 and was completed seven months later. All bar 250 miles saw the Range Rovers pounding down passable roads with the Darien Gap section of the journey taking 99 days to complete. Both vehicles suffered breakdowns including broken half-shafts and a secondhand 88-inch Land Rover was purchased in Panama to help. The expedition was hindered by heavy rains that fell later in the season than normal and aluminium ladders and inflatable boats had to be utilised to cross several rivers.

The expedition was crewed by military personnel and the Range Rovers were modified to allow a single reclining seat to replace the traditional rear bench seat so that the drivers could take it in turns to sleep. These vehicles have been preserved in this condition, apart from receiving new chassis, as the originals were removed and cut up by engineers who studied them to note any signs of stress.

Another venture was the Joint Services Expedition in 1975 that saw four 101s cross Africa. Led by RAF Squadron Leader

Tom Sheppard, the quartet of one-tonne vehicles covered the 7,494 miles eastward from the Atlantic coast to the Red Sea in just 100 days. The mission proved a resounding success and the military 101s entered service the following year.

The Camel Trophy was one of the most successful events in the history of Land Rover. Although only three entrants took part in the inaugural 1980 competition – and they were all from West Germany and had chosen to drive Jeeps – Land Rover soon took on the sponsorship of the event and provided the vehicles for each country that had agreed to participate. The number of entrants ranged from 12 to 18 over the years and the competition was staged in such inhospitable places as Borneo, Siberia and Mongolia. Such was the spirit of the event that teams could win awards for helping out their fellow competitors as they found themselves having to winch their vehicles up steep inclines and making rafts from whatever materials were to hand in order to traverse rivers. Various models were supplied during Land Rover's association with the competition from 1981 to 1998 including Range Rovers, Series IIIs, Discoverys and Freelanders.

Following Land Rover's decision not to continue with the Camel Trophy amid concerns about damaging the environment the competitors were travelling through, the company launched the G4 Challenge in 2003. This was intended to attract customers who had so far resisted the temptation of owning a Land Rover (in whatever guise) and was not limited to driving one of the supplied 4x4s. Instead, competitors had to demonstrate all-round skills including orienteering, kayaking, mountain biking and abseiling. Held in four different areas of the world, Land Rover used the event as a PR exercise and different models were provided depending on the brand the company wanted to promote in that territory. The 2003 Challenge saw Defenders, Discoverys, Range Rovers and Freelanders being used, and the ordinary customer on the street was also able to feel part of the event once special edition models were introduced into the showrooms.

Rallying has also played a large part in the company's history. The final year of the 1970s saw the inaugural Paris to Dakar Rally being staged and the French

LEFT The Land Rover G4 Challenge is the ultimate driving adventure

pairing of Alain Génestier and Joseph Terbiaut won in their privately entered Range Rover. The gruelling 6,213-mile race through some of Africa's harshest terrain proved to be the perfect setting for the luxury saloon and their feat was emulated by compatriots René Metge and Bernard Giroux two years later. While Land Rover have never officially entered a works team into the rally, they did unofficially endorse and support a French entry between 1983 and 1986. The Halt'Up! entry was barely recognisable as a Range Rover, however, with the traditional body being replaced by a carbon fibre shell more suited to the demands of the rally. The last victory for any Range Rover entry proved to be 1981 and the race has been dominated in recent years by Mitsubishi's Pajero. Thankfully, then-Prime Minister Margaret Thatcher's son Mark was not driving a Land Rover entry when he, his co-driver and mechanic lost their way in their Peugeot 504 and were listed as missing for six days in 1982!

Thankfully, Drew Bowler never suffered this fate with his Bowler Wildcat. This was a specialised rally vehicle constructed from Land Rover components that competed in various coun-

tries such as Australia, Russia and the United Arab Emirates. Each vehicle was built to the customer's individual specifications so no two models were ever the same. The Wildcat earned a well-respected reputation among the

rallying community and Land Rover officially sponsored the Bowler team during the 2002-03 season.

Although the company have never officially raced their Freelander, they did supply half a dozen specially pre-pared vehicles to support the Ford team entry into the Kenyan leg of the 2001 World Rally Championship. Following the competition, one of the cars was donated to the British Rally Championship as a safety car.

Chapter 20

Facts & Trivia

Land Rover hits 4,000,000

SUCH IS THE LAND ROVER'S success and enduring popularity over the seven decades since its introduction that May 2007 saw the four millionth such branded vehicle roll off the production lines. This Discovery 3 was donated to the Born Free Foundation that had first been set up in 1984 as Zoo Check by Virginia McKenna and Bill

RIGHT Noel Edmonds in a Range Rover

FAR RIGHT Land Rover history goes back to 1861

Travers. The couple had portrayed husband and wife team naturalist Joy and game warden George Adamson in the 1966 film Born Free that told the story of lioness Elsa and her cubs.

Land Rover evolves from sewing machine

IF YOU TRACE THE LAND ROVER ancestry back far enough you will find that it is distantly related to the sewing machine. The first Rover was a tricycle manufactured by Starley and Sutton Company of Coventry, England in 1883; the company had been founded by John Kemp Starley and William Sutton five years earlier. Starley had formerly worked with his uncle, James Starley, (father of the cycle trade) who began manufacturing sewing machines in 1861 before switching to bicycles eight years later. The Rover Motor Company name was, of course, adopted in 1904 – three years after Starley's death – and the rest, as they say, is history…

The ultimate accessory

EVEN WHEN YOURE NOT SAT behind the wheel of your Land Rover, you can still show your allegiance to the marque thanks to a range of accessories and gifts. These include hats, clothing, key chains, bottle openers, teddy bears, 3D lapel badges as well as signs that forbid other cars to park in the space reserved for your pride and joy.

Did you know?

IT IS CLAIMED THAT THE LAND Rover is the first vehicle of any kind to be seen by 60 percent of the population in the developing world!

Mad Max

SUCH WAS THE SECRECY WITH which Land Rover carried out its trials and testing of the new Freelander in 1996 that the proposed vehicles were heavily disguised as Maestro vans.

FACTS & TRIVIA

RIGHT AND FAR
RIGHT Dakar Kit cars
in off-road action

The test drivers affectionately nicknamed these prototypes "Mad Max".

Just the kit!

DAKAR CARS LTD OF KENT HAVE filled a void in the marketplace for owners who have trashed their Range Rovers beyond economical repair while competing off-road. The Dakar four-wheel drive is a kit car based on a Range Rover chassis and running gear.

Happy 60th birthday

A UNIQUE EVENT ORGANISED TO celebrate the 60th Anniversary of Land Rover. Took place on 21-24 March 2008, Land Rover fans from across the world in Cooma, Australia to celebrate the grand old lady of 4x4s becoming a pensioner.

The Snowy Mountains saw similar celebrations in 1988 and 1998 and was chosen as the venue because it is generally agreed that the Land Rover came to prominence in Australia in the 1950s when it was one of the major vehicles

used during the construction of the Snowy Mountains Hydro Scheme. Events planned for the weekend include guest speakers and event trials with hundreds of specimens being on display.

The concept

THE 2004 NORTH AMERICAN International Auto Show in Detroit saw history in the making as Land Rover unveiled its first ever concept show car. The Range Stormer was a high performance, sports tourer SUV concept car, which showcased a future design direction for the company.

The brand

THE RANGE ROVER BRAND has also expanded into bicycle production endorsement, pushchair manufacture licensing as well as interests in coffee in the form of the Land Rover Coffee Company.

Sponsorship

WITH A GLOBALLY RENOWNED brand, Land Rover is a supporter and major sponsor of several high-profile sports.

Rugby

Rugby and the ethos of Land Rover go hand-in-hand and both share similar values: integrity, courage, pride, composure and capability. As sponsors of the sport encompassing all levels from the Land Rover Premiership Rugby Cup for under 11 and under 12 teams to Premiership Rugby, Land Rover are particularly proud to be sponsors of the 2013 British & Irish Lions Tour to Australia and Hong Kong, as well as being a Worldwide Partner of the

Rugby World Cup for 2015.

Skiing

The Land Rover is the official vehicle of the Ski Club of Great Britain and the company also sponsor all of the Ski Club's on-snow activity.

Equestrian

Land Rover is proud sponsors of eques-

trianism from the British Eventing Team to the Burghley Horse Trials and the Royal Windsor Horse Show.

Sailing

Land Rover have for the first time become major sponsors of the Extreme Sailing Series in a three-year deal that has given a real boost to the shift towards stadium racing in the competitive sailing world.

Chapter 21

Association of Land Rover Clubs

Single Marque Clubs

101 F.C.C.& R. (101 Forward Control Club and Register)
www.101club.org

Discovery Owners Club
www.discoveryownersclub.org

LR Series I Club
www.lrsoc.com

LR Series II Club
www.series2club.co.uk

Lightweight LR Club

LR Register (48-53)
www.landrover-register1948-53.org.uk

The Camel Club
www.cameltrophy.co.uk

The G4 Owners Club
www.g4ownersclub.com

Local Area Clubs

Anglian LRC
www.anglianlrc.com

Aylesbury LR Fanatics Club

Breckland LRC

www.brecklandlrc.com

Cheltenham & Cotswold ROC

Chiltern Vale LRC
www.cvlrc.co.uk

Cornwall & Devon LRC
www.cornwallanddevonland-roverclub.co.uk

Cumbrian ROC (N.W.) Ltd.
www.crocweb.co.uk

Dorset Land Rover Club Ltd.
http://dorsetrover.co.uk

ASSOCIATION OF LAND ROVER CLUBS

Dunsfold Collection Southern
Social Section
www.dunsfoldcollection.co.uk

East Northants LROC
www.enlroc.co.uk/wp

Essex LRC
www.elrc.info

Hants & Berks LRO
www.hbro.co.uk

Lancs & Cheshire LROC
www.rovertorque.com

Leics & Rutland LRC
www.lrlrc.co.uk

Lincolnshire LRC
www.llrc.co.uk

Merseyside LROC
www.mlroc.co.uk

Midland ROC
www.mroc.co.uk

North East ROC
www.nero.org.uk

North Wales LRC
www.nwlrc.co.uk

Nottingham LRC

Peak & Dukeries LRC
www.panddlrc.co.uk

Red Rose LRC
www.landroverclub.co.uk

Scottish LROC
http://slroc2.co.uk

Somerset & Wilts LRC
https://sites.google.com/site/
swlandrover/home

South Coast LROC

Southern ROC
www.sroc.co.uk

Staffs & Shrops LRC
www.saslrc.co.uk

Wye & Welsh LRC
www.wyeandwelshlrc.co.uk

Yorkshire LROC
www.ylroc.co.uk

Overseas Clubs

Dansk Land Rover Klub
www.dlrk.dk

Deutscher Land Rover-Club eV
www.deutscher-land-rover-club.de

Dutch L.R. Register
www.dlrr.nl

Land Rover Classic Club
www.lrcc.de

Land Rover Registro Storico
Italiano
www.registrostoricolandrover.eu

Land-Rovers of Switzerland
www.lros.ch

Norsk Land Rover Klubb
www.nlrk.no

Pacific Coast Rover Club
http://pcrc.net/Default.
aspx?tabid=36

Swedish Land Rover Klubb
www.slrk.org/svensk-land-
rover-klubb

ABOVE Association of
Land Rover Clubs logo

Chapter 22

The Land Rover Defender R.I.P

SINCE THIS BOOK WAS FIRST published, Jaguar Land Rover has announced that it will stop production of its Defender model in 2015 because it will not meet new European laws on fuel emissions.

The last of the 4x4 models will roll off the production line at its plant in Solihull in the West Midlands in December 2015 after an evolution of more than 67 years.

The first model in the style of the Defender was introduced in 1948 and was modelled on a World War II Jeep. It was not given the Defender name until the early 1990s, shortly after the launch of the Discovery and has sold more than two million around the world since then.

Plans by the European Council and Parliament to bring in stricter measures for new car emissions by 2020 meant there were environmental conditions the Defender just wouldn't meet. A "instantly recognisable " replacement model for the Defender is being developed for launch in 2016.

Auto Express magazine editor Steve Fowler said the model had taken on "iconic status" after being driven by members of the Royal Family and being featured in the latest James Bond film, Skyfall.

"It's a very important market for Land Rover, one of its three pillars with the Range Rover and the Discovery. As

ABOVE The Land Rover Defender

we experienced with another iconic car, the Mini, it had a bit of a sabbatical before coming back and that's what I fully expect to happen with the Defender," he added.

A disappointed Frank King, from the Land Rover owners' club in Cannock, commented: "The silhouette still looks the same as it did 67 years ago, although its been upgraded and had new engines and whatever. It's a real shame to see it go."

The pictures in this book were provided courtesy of the following:

GETTY IMAGES
101 Bayham Street, London NW1 0AG

SHUTTERSTOCK IMAGES
www.shutterstock.com

NATIONAL MOTOR MUSEUM TRUST
Beaulieu, Brockenhurst, Hampshire SO42 7ZN

WIKIMEDIA COMMONS

Design and artwork by: Scott Giarnese

Published by: G2 Entertainment Limited

Publishers: Jules Gammond and Edward Adams

Foreword by: Stephen Vokins